Food For The Soul

Diet of a Yogi

Sundari Dasi

Library of Congress Control Number: 2019902433

ISBN: 978-1-64516-049-6

Printed in the United States by Morris Publishing®
3212 East Highway 30
Kearney, NE 68847
1-800-650-7888

DISCLAIMER

We have used our best efforts in preparing the "Food For The Soul" recipe book. All material in the Food For The Soul recipe Book is provided for your information only and is not be construed as medical advice or instruction. No action or inaction should be taken based solely on the contents of this information; instead, readers should consult appropriate health professionals on any matter relating to their health and well-being. We do NOT claim to be doctors, nutritionists or dietitians. The information in the Food For the Soul recipe book is merely our personal opinion and does not replace professional or nutritional advice.

Food Handling

Please use great caution and sanitary practices when handling food products. Refer to your health department's safe food handling guidelines. Wash your hands and surfaces thoroughly before and after handling any food product.

We expressly disclaim responsibility for any adverse effect that may result from the use or application of the information contained in the Food For the Soul recipe book.

Testimonials

Testimonials, and examples found for the Food For the soul recipe book have been submitted to us by those who have participated and followed our yoga and fasting programs. Every person has a unique experiences, eating habits, and applies the information differently. Thus, the experiences that we share from other people may not reflect the typical purchaser's experience, may not apply to the average person and are not intended to represent or guarantee that anyone will achieve the same or similar results.

Table of Contents

01 Foreword and Introduction

All of the 100 recipes are Vegan Plant based, with 14 having vegetarian options. Out of 100 recipes 94 are gluten free . Please refer to gluten and vegetarian options page in the end for details.

02 Nourish and Detox with Lemonades

03 Herbal Teas

Table of Contents

04 Silken Smoothies

05 Art of Sprouting

06 Apple Sauce

Table of Contents

Table of Contents

Table of Contents

13 Wonder Recipes

14 15 Day Fasting Meal Plan

Foreword

Food For The Soul – Diet Of A Yogi

First is Food! First is Character! These two traditional Vedic maxims are essential components for a healthy body and mental equilibrium that will in turn help create a harmonious, happy family and social life. Alas, modern society has discarded these wise precepts, and we can now witness the results.

Today, more than 2 in 3 adults in the United States are considered overweight or obese. More than one-third of children ages 6 to 19 are also considered overweight or obese.

The growth of fast food in America seems to coincide with the growth of obesity. The Obesity Action Coalition (OAC) reports that the number of fast food restaurants in America has doubled since 1970. The number of obese Americans has also more than doubled.
https://www.healthline.com/health/fast-food-effects-on-body#effects-on-society

An unhealthy diet is one of the significant risk factors for a range of chronic diseases, including cardiovascular diseases, cancer, diabetes and other conditions linked to obesity. Specific recommendations for a healthy diet include: eating more fruit, vegetables, legumes, nuts, and grains; cutting down on salt, sugar, and fats. It is also advisable to choose unsaturated fats, instead of saturated fats and towards the elimination of trans-fatty acids.
Clearly wholesome food, balanced diet, and sound character go hand in hand and must be restored at all cost.

In her new book, Food For The Soul – Diet of a Yogi, author Sundari Dasi touches the heart of the matter by elaborating on how fasting, lifestyle, good food, and good health go together. These wholesome recipes are a product of years of research and anyone who has tried them, tasted them have been mesmerized and benefited by them. These recipes are designed to heal the body as well as the mind and foster yoga and meditational practices. This book has fantastic fasting detox lemonades, smoothies, post fasting soups, sprouts, salads and much more. For it is not only the quality of the food that is essential but indeed the quality of consciousness of one preparing such food.

Being a practicing yogini for many years as well as a committed vegetarian, Sundari Dasi is well equipped to present to her readers the secrets of healthy and wholesome life through her numerous nutritious recipes. She expertly blends the traditional and the modern by introducing innovative preparations as well as a scientifically balanced diet. Her book is a must for all those who are serious about restoring their health at all levels.

H H Bhakti Raghava Swami
Nityananda Trayodasi
Feb 17th, 2019,
Mayapur, India.

Authors Note

Yoga is not just a practice but a complete lifestyle. An essential aspect of this lifestyle is fasting and healthy diet. Although many books are available on the yoga asanas hardly any book is available that gives us food for fasting, cleansing and post fasting. The benefits of practicing yoga, meditation, fasting, cleansing can only be maintained by regular fasting and diet. After having cooked for yogis at Yoga retreats, Meditation retreats and for my husband who would fast regularly I decided to pen all the research into an excellent cookbook beneficial to all but especially catered to the yogis. This book is based on yoga and ayurvedic texts.

The idea of writing "Food For The Soul" is not to just create another delicious cookbook but a book to assist you in conscious health and spiritual journey.

Wishing you all a happy, healthy "Food For Your Soul."

Sundari Dasi

Introduction

Food for the soul is a plant based vegan cookbook with Vegetarian option, designed to assist you in fasting, cleansing or post fasting maintenance of health. Even if you are not fasting the recipes here are very healthy and help you maintain good health. Those practicing Yoga or looking for healthy food options will love this book. The book begins with lemonades which are very beneficial for fasting, keeping ourselves hydrated or aid in weight loss.

Excellent hot herbal teas are the next section. Hot herbal teas get your circulation going. When infused with proper herbs teas can have a magical medicinal effect on the mind and body.

The next section on smoothies is a carefully crafted combination of fruits and nuts which are very nutritious and very delectable. They are midway between a full fast or a full meal but are very filling, keeping us light and active.

After detoxing lemonades, herbs, and smoothies, we present sprouts and salads as a wholesome, juicy and healthy means of building up your strength. Sprouts are full of life energy, *prana*. When slightly cooked and combined with delicious salads and mouthwatering dressing, it can become a full super food meal!

A stand-alone apple sauce is an excellent, easy dish for any day. Fasting or not apple sauce is very special.

Yogic scriptures say food should be easy to digest. Soups are in one sense ready to digest food. Hot, full of energy and easily circulate in the body, soups are good on any given day.

Frying is generally not considered to be healthy. However, it tastes good. One can get the same taste with baking. The next section Baking Over Frying has baked banana, falafel, samosa, quinoa super food burger, and asparagus baked which makes this section very interesting.

Food is eaten in combinations, like salad with salad dressings, burgers with sauce and dips and so on. In our Chakra Chutney Corner, we introduce several chutneys that are good with any food, very healthy and delectable.

Cleansing is the beginning of yoga practices. To attain and maintain good results of cleansing, khichris are the best dishes. Very simple and easy to make, we have added super food quinoa to the khichris.

Radiant rice section is full of wonderful rice recipes. These range from sweet Blueberry rice to traditional Lali lemon rice. Wild rice is considered very nutritious, and we have included a wild rice stir-fry. Check out this section for rice wonders.

Finally, we introduce "Wonder Recipes" These wonder recipes range from simple chips to healthy pizzas. Vegetable Spaghetti, veggie burgers, jack fruit burgers included we have tried our best to be innovative in turning regular dishes into healthy, tasty eats. This section also includes Moringa super food splatters which are a very special way of having a super food. Since we are from south India, we have some unique south Indian dishes which are tasty and healthy in themselves, presented here with a personal touch.

All in all these 100 recipes are our hard and heartfelt efforts to bring about good health to all of you.

The Importance of Fasting and Proper Diet

Food is life, the *Taittariya Upanishad* states that everything is a transformation of food. Matter transforms based on who mingles with it. Same dirt turns into a variety of plants and fruits depending on which species they get connected to. Interestingly all variety of plants and animals have various types of immunity and defense mechanisms which they develop with an instinct to protect themselves against diseases. For, e.g., A cat when sick will fast and eat some medicinal grass which it can find and heal itself. Similarly, other animals find a means to treat themselves or have mechanisms of defense and survival.

Humans, however, are gifted with knowledge of the ancient sciences like Yoga, Ayurveda, traditional herbs and medicines from the old folklore in various parts of the world. One such miracle medicine mentioned in all yogic, as well as all religious scriptures which helps us heal, is "fasting." There is nothing more effective than "fasting" in terms of rejuvenating our body and mind.

The Vedic texts explain fasting methods like "*Chandrayana Vrata*" or   fasting based on the moon cycle. By fasting according to the sequence of the moon, freedom from *karma* and disease is obtained. There is also fasting   mentioned on *Ekadasi*, the 11th day of the moon cycle which is very beneficial for the mind and body alike. These and many more fasting methods give us immense benefits. There have been scientific studies conducted on the   benefits of short term and long-term water fasting. They have produced incredible results, and people have been able to cure and reverse many chronic health conditions. The only challenge is to maintain the benefits after the fasting period is done.

There is a need to keep proper nutrition for the rest of our lives. Only by a proper diet and exercise, will we be able to be consistently healthy.

How Fasting Works

When you want to clean a machine, you turn it off, clean it and service it. Similarly, the body is a machine that needs to be serviced and to do that, it needs some well deserved "rest". Fasting achieves that purpose.

Let me give you another e.g. When we suffer from a fracture, we protect the fractured part of the body with some plaster and hold the element in place with a sling or so. We are resting the body part which in turn activates the self-healing mechanism and heals the body part. Similarly, if we provide our entire body with proper rest, then the whole system has an opportunity to heal itself. If we simply keep eating three meals a day and not give the body enough rest, our bodies are in a constant "digestive" mode and the body does not get enough rest to rejuvenate itself. By fasting and at the same time by drinking detoxifying lemonades, we provide the body with rest and an outlet to the toxins in the body. Even according to Ayurveda fasting is very beneficial and helps the body in higher levels of digestion and eliminates toxins.

The Fire Of Digestion According To Ayurveda

There are seven digestive fires in the body according to Ayurveda. Food that we eat is broken down and becomes *rasa* or plasma tissue, then it is converted to rakta or blood, blood is further digested and converted to *mamsa* or muscles. Muscles are further digested and converted to *medas* or fat, Fat is absorbed and turned to *asti* or bones and bones are also digested and converted to *majja* or bone marrow and finally bone marrow is converted to either semen or *ojas* (higher mental energy) . This digestion is aided by the seven *agnis* or fires which cook the food from one form to the other. This digestion in the body is continuously going on. There needs to be sufficient time and catalysts for all these levels of metabolism to take place.

When we are continuously eating, we are in the lower rungs of digestion, and the body does not have enough time or energy for the higher levels of metabolism, i.e. muscles, bones and so on. It requires a lot of exercise, proper diet and an excellent mood to activate the higher levels of digestion.

Fasting combined with yoga or exercise is the best way to enable the higher level of digestion. When we fast, the excess fats accumulated over a period of time breaks down and gets digested into muscles and bones. Hence fasting is the best method to reduce fat and increase muscles and, when adequately directed we get more mental energy. For attaining deeper states of yogic meditation, fasting followed by eating appropriate food prescribed in the yogic and ayurvedic texts is recommended.

Fasting is beneficial to all except those who have some serious physical injury. Fasting is essential to convert these stored fats into energy and get the best out of our body.

Food For The Soul attempts to provide recipes during fasts for detoxification. Smoothies, sprouts soups and much more to gradually build up your diet after fast and special healthy wonder recipes for a healthy eating on a regular basis. Our recipes are designed to help you to detox and maintain all the good results you obtain by fasting, exercise, yoga and meditation.

Lemonades

Lemonades are excellent for fasting, to detox or to lose weight. They are very alkaline and keep the body refreshed. In general, the alkaline body is useful to prevent diseases. An acidic body is very prone to infections.

Lime is a rich source of vitamin C and boosts the immune system. Lemonades are also a digestive and a detoxifying agent. They also help to cleanse the liver leading to better health.

Lemonades during fast help keep the body hydrated and at the same time digest excess fat in the body. The benefits of fasting can be substantially observed when we fast on lemonades for at least 3-4 days. By that time body would be beginning to digest the reserve fats in the body and gradually reducing the accumulated fats and toxins.

However, to survive for a few days without eating any solid food at the same time fight hunger, one needs to feel full (not hungry), comfortable and hydrated. Lime juice mixed with chia seeds acts like a miracle in this regard.

Along with the above benefits, Lime's anti-inflammatory properties help in fighting respiratory tract infections, sore throat in addition to reducing aches and pains in the body. In our   detoxifying lemonades note that all   lemonades are along with soaked chia seeds and we have added some fruit juices which give additional benefits. By detoxifying the body, digestion naturally increases and it balances all other functions like blood pressure, excretion and so on.

So Why Did We Select Chia Seeds?

Chia is a magic seed, and its meaning originates from the Mayan word "strength." Chia seeds are highly nutrient (in proteins) and give us the necessary amount of energy to fast, keeps us hydrated and helps us beat hunger. At the same time, it also detoxifies the entire body and replenishes the kidneys. It's a super food which was popular in ancient times and is recently gaining popularity again. They are mostly grown organic and gluten-free.

Chia seeds have tons of fiber helping it pass through the digestive system quickly. This quality of chia seeds also helps in weight loss. Other benefits include balancing blood sugars, providing bone nutrients and fighting inflammation. Lemonades help keep body alkaline, chia seeds hydrate the body and supply the required nutrients for fasting.

Fruits Included In Our Lemonades And Their Benefits

Kiwi

Kiwi is alkaline in nature and a good source of vitamin C. It is rich in fibers and helps in digestion, aids in proper bowel movements and is also known to induce sleep. Rich in foliate, vitamins, and minerals like potassium and magnesium.

Blueberries

Blueberries are the most popular berries mainly for their taste and nutrients. Known as the king of anti-oxidant fruits they are low in calories but high in nutrients like vitamin K. They are good at cell repair and protect against aging. Blueberries can also regulate blood pressure.

Strawberries

Strawberries are a rich source of anti-oxidants and fiber. They support the immune system. Strawberries are a good aid to weight loss. Known to have good anti-micro bacterial effects. They relieve constipation and relieve stress.

Pineapples

Pineapples are rich in antioxidants and enzymes which fight inflammation. They fight cold and throat infection. Pineapples contain bromelain, a group of digestive enzymes that breaks down proteins and help us digest them.

Nectarines

Nectarines like other fresh fruits are rich in fiber which make them ideal for weight loss. Nectarines are excellent sources of beta-carotene, vitamin C, and lutein. They enhance immunity, protect vision, and prevent numerous diseases.

Mint

Mint who's active component is menthol is a breath freshner and helps with oral health. Furthermore mint has antiseptic and antibacterial properties that relieves of indigestion.

Ginger

Ayurveda explains that ginger can be consumed fresh or as dry powder both of which are highly beneficial. Ginger is best known for promoting digestion and help eliminate waste from the body. It is diaphoretic, which means that it promotes sweating, working to warm the body from within. Ginger also helps reduce inflammation in the body. Ginger promotes digestion so well that it can help balance blood sugar levels.

Raspberry

Rich in fiber **Raspberry** is known to help prevent constipation and to maintain a healthy digestive tract. High in vitamin C, raspberries promote eye health. It helps make skin better and balances sugar

Blackberries like raspberry are rich in fibers and similar in properties to raspberry. They're packed with vitamin C, vitamin K and blackberries are rich in manganese.

Turmeric

Turmeric is a wonder herb and may be the most effective nutritional supplement in existence. Turmeric has powerful medicinal properties because of the presence of compounds called curcuminoids, the most important of which is curcumin. It has potent anti-inflammatory effects and is a powerful antioxidant, boosts brain growth and lowers risk of heart disease. Turmeric adds immense flavor and promotes digestion.

Herbs Used In Our Tea Section

Herbs have a digestive and uplifting effect. By drinking hot herbal teas the mucus lining of the body becomes light, blood circulation is improved and fire of digestion is activated. Herbal teas act as a catalyst to ignite the fire.

In the herbal teas section you will learn how to make best use of the spices that are already in your pantry and make wonderful herbal teas and infusions which are not only magical in adding flavor to your hot or cold beverages, but they are also very useful serving as wonderful home remedies.

Fennel

Fennel is a concentrated source of minerals like Copper, Potassium, Calcium, Zinc, Manganese, Vitamin C, Iron, Selenium and Magnesium. Fennel is known to regulate blood pressure and also help in water retention. Its very beneficial for those who have diabetes, asthma, gas troubles and congestion. It is a wonder herb for breastfeeding moms.

Cumin

Cumin is antiseptic and a diuretic. It helps diabetics by detoxifying the body and helps reduce cholesterol. It promotes digestion and is a rich source of Iron. Since it detoxifies the body cumin is also known to help in weight loss.
Cumin seeds reduce aches and pains in the body.

Cardamom

Cardamom is an antioxidant with diuretic properties. It aids digestion, eliminates bad breath and prevents cavities. It is anti-bacterial and treats infections.
Its an aromatic herb and this aroma is known to reduce insomnia. Cardamom is known to be very helpful in overcoming constipation.

Cinnamon and Cloves

Cinnamon and cloves are nice warming herbs which boost your digestive system and also open up the sinuses and reduce the mucus secretion in the body. Cinnamon is known to balance blood sugar levels.

Chamomile

Many people enjoy chamomile tea as a caffeine-free alternative to black or green tea and for its earthy, slightly sweet taste. It is known to aid digestion and sleep. It has anti-oxidants and anti-inflammatory properties. These two properties help in variety of health conditions including heart diseases, diarrhea and stomach ulcers.

Detox

Lemonades

Golden Kiwi Chia Mint Detox

Ingredients (servings 2)

3 ripe golden Kiwi peeled and chopped

1/2 cup mint leaves

Fresh juice of 1 squeezed lime

2 tbsp Chia seeds soaked overnight in 3 cups of water

2 Tablespoon maple syrup (optional)

Steps

1. Blend the chopped kiwi, mint and lime with a cup of water in a blender and pour it into a jar.

2. Now add the overnight soaked chia seeds and the maple syrup, stir well (breaking chia seed lumps) and your Golden Kiwi chia detox lemonade is ready.

Ginger Mint Chia Detox

Ingredients (servings 2)

2 inch piece of ginger

1 cup of mint leaves

Fresh juice of 1 lime

2 tablespoon Chia seeds

in 3 cups of water soaked

overnight

2 Tablespoon maple syrup

(optional)

Steps

1. Blend the chopped ginger and mint with freshly squeezed lime with a cup of water in a blender. Now pour it into a jar

2. Add two cups of water and two tablespoon of maple syrup. Now add the overnight soaked chia seeds and stir well (breaking chia seed lumps) and your Ginger mint chia detox lemonade is ready.

Raspberry Blackberry Chia

Ingredients (servings 3)

1 cup of raspberry

1 cup of blackberries

2 tablespoons of lime juice squeezed

2 tablespoons of chia seeds soaked
overnight in 3 cups of water

2 tablespoons of maple syrup
(optional)

Steps

1. Blend the fresh blackberry, raspberry
with 2 cups of water and lime in a blender
and pour it into a jar.

2. Now add the overnight soaked chia
seeds and maple syrup, stir well (breaking chia seed lumps) and your Berry Chia
detox lemonade is ready.

Blueberry/Strawberry Chia

Ingredients

1 cup of fresh blueberry fruit

Fresh juice of 1 squeezed lime

3 cups of spring water

2 tablespoons of maple syrup
(optional)

Steps

1. Blend in the blueberry/strawberry in 2 cups of water with freshly squeezed lime in a blender. Now pour it into a jar.

2. Now add the overnight soaked chia seeds, maple syrup and stir well (breaking chia seed lumps) and your Blueberry/Strawberry chia detox lemonade is ready.

25

Mango Mint Detox

Ingredients (servings 2)

2 cups of ripe mango chopped

1 tablespoon of dried mint leaves

2 tablespoons of Chia seeds soaked

overnight in 3 cups of water

Fresh juice of 1 squeezed lime

2 tablespoons of maple syrup

(optional)

Steps

1. Blend the fresh mango, dried mint and lime with 2 cups of water in a blender.

2. Now add the overnight soaked chia seeds and maple syrup, stir well and your Mango mint chia detox lemonade is ready.

Pineapple Chia Detox

Ingredients

2 cups of chopped pineapple

Fresh juice of 1 squeezed lime

2 tablespoons Chia seeds soaked

overnight in 3 cups of water

½ cup maple syrup (optional)

Steps

1. Blend the chopped fresh pineapples with the fresh lime juice together

2. Dilute this solution with 3 cups of water and add the   maple syrup and the Chia seeds Mix well (breaking chia seed lumps) and the Pineapple chia detox lemonade drink is ready

Lets get tropical with pineapples !!!

Nectarine Chia Detox

Adding a special nectarine flavour to your detox fast.

Ingredients (servings 2)

2 fully ripe nectarine peeled and chopped into four

Fresh juice of 1 squeezed lime

½ cup maple syrup)optionsl)

2 tablespoon chia seeds soaked overnight

Steps

1. Blend in the chopped nectarine and lime with a cup of water in a blender. Now pour it into a jar.

2. Add two cups of water and two tbsp of maple syrup . Now add the overnight soaked chia seeds (breaking chia seed lumps), stir well and your Nectarine chia detox lemonade is ready.

Turmeric Chia Detox

There is no herb like turmeric. Try this and experience !

Turmeric Chia Detox

Ingredients (servings 2)

1 tbsp organic turmeric powder
4 cardamom pods
Fresh juice of 1 squeezed lime
2 tablespoon Chia seeds soaked overnight
2 tablespoons of maple syrup (optional

Steps

1. Blend in turmeric powder and cardamom pods with freshly squeezed lime with a cup of water in a blender. Now pour it into a jar.
2. Add two cups of water and two tbsp of maple syrup. Now add the overnight soaked chia seeds and stir well (breaking chia seed lumps) and your Turmeric chia detox lemonade is ready.

Green Shakti

Ingredients (servings 2)

1 cup of cilantro
1 cucumber peeled and sliced
1 tablespoon of coconut oil
1/2 cup of parsley
2 teaspoon of lime juice

Steps

1. Powerblend the ingredients together with a cup of water until you see no layer of greens and oils   separated as shown in the image.

Green Shakti

Greens are cleansing, refreshing and energizing

Energizing Herbal teas

Cumin Fennel Tea

Nothing like cumin to cleanse

Servings 2

Cooktime 20 mins

Ingredients

3 teaspoons of cumin seeds

3 teaspoons of fennel seeds

Steps

1. Bring 5 cups of water to boil in a skillet then add both the spices and turn the heat to medium.

2. Let it simmer for at least 15 minutes on low heat. Now a nice aromatic cumin fennel tea is ready. It tastes amazing, but if you would like it to be sweet you may add a teaspoon of maple syrup or honey.

Turmeric Spice Tea
An antibiotic cleansing tea

Servings 2

Cooktime 15 mins

Ingredients (servings 2)

1-inch freshly grated ginger

1/2 teaspoon turmeric powder

5 cardamom pods

1 teaspoon lime

Steps

1. Bring 5 cups of water to boil in a skillet then add cardamom, turmeric and ginger

2. Let it simmer for at 5-8 mins on low heat.

3. Turn off the heat and squeeze the fresh lime and serve hot.

Energising Refreshing Tea

Cardamom is best known to get your circulation going

Servings 2

Cooktime 12 mins

Ingredients

4-5 fresh mint leaves

5 cardamom pods

2 inch bark of cinnamon

Steps

1. Boil 5 cups of water in a medium size skillet.

2. Now add cinnamon and cardamom pods

3. Let it simmer on low heat for 5-8 minutes

Turn off the heat and serve with fresh mint leaves

Cardamom Chamomile Tea

The best of all teas chamomile

Servings 3

Cooktime 15 mins

Ingredients

1/2 cup of dried chamomile flowers

6-8 cardamom pods

1/2 a teaspoon of cardamom powder

Steps

1. Boil all the ingredients in 8 cups of water. Now simmer for 8-10 minutes.

Strain it and divide it into 3 equal portions. Drink it in the morning, evening and night for good results. Repeat it for 3 days. It is the best kidney cleanser.

Orange Zest Tea

Ingredients

2 slices of Orange

2 inch cinnamon stick

2 cardamom pods

Steps

1. Boil 2 inch cinnamon stick and cardamom in 5 cups of water for 5 minutes on low heat.

2. Then turn off the heat, add the fresh orange zest.

3. While serving in the cup add a sliced thin piece of orange on the top as shown in the image, it's a wonderful energizing refreshing drink anytime in the day.

Lets get tangy with some Orange tea

Servings 2

Cooktime 10 mins

Ginger Fennel Tea

Servings 2

Cooktime 8 mins

Ingredients

1/2 inch ginger

1 tablespoon fennel

1-inch stick of cinnamon

1 tablespoon of cumin

Steps

1. Boil all ingredients in 6 cups of water. Then let it simmer for about 8 minutes.

2. Then turn off the heat.

Serve hot

Turmeric Fennel Tea

Ingredients

2 tablespoons of fennel

1/4 teaspoon of turmeric

1 teaspoon of lime freshly

squeezed

Steps

1. Boil the fennel in 8-10 cups of water. Then simmer for about 8-10 mins.

2. Turn off the heat and let it steep for 5 mins.

3. Now add the turmeric and fresh lime juice, stir well, serve hot. Servings 3

41

SILKEN SMOOTHIES

Smoothies

Building up your diet after a fast or trying to get out of an eating disorder like overeating can be best done with the help of fruits. Fruits are neither too light nor too heavy and serve as an in-between medium to come out of a fasting regimen or reduce our regular food intake.

After a fasting marathon one should not eat grains and heavy foods right away, one must gradually bring the body to an optimum level of digestion by either fresh fruits or smoothies. Although fresh fruits are the best for consumption, smoothies are more attractive as we can flavor them with different combinations, juicier and adding soaked nuts makes them even more nutritious. Fruits are refreshing, healthy and light. Smoothies are the best productive things to have in all seasons except the winter. Fruits also provide us with tons of essential nutrients. The best time to have a smoothie is around midday as *pitta*, or digestive heat is optimum around that time. To have it very early or very late in the day can increase the mucus in the body. Fruits are a good source of various vitamins and minerals. A proper combination of fruits though is essential to derive the best nutrients from a smoothie. A wrong combination or too many fruits or mixing fruits with milk or yogurt will not give the desired effect in digestion. The focus of Ayurveda or yoga is to make the food easily digestible giving the best possible nutrients. Fruits, dry fruits and nuts are the right combinations. Do not add any sugar to the smoothies. Maple syrup is recommended if you would like to have it little sweeter.

Here we present the best possible combinations which we produced after much research.

The texture of the smoothies makes them more delectable. To maintain the consistency of smoothies, i.e., to make them silky smooth we add bananas. They are not only soft and retain the texture, but are rich in fiber as well.

Bananas

Extremely healthy and delicious. Rich in fiber, antioxidants and several nutrients. Rich in pectin and resistant starch which help relieve hunger. They help overcome muscle cramps and fatigue due to exercise. Bananas aid weight loss because they're low in calories and high in nutrients and fiber. Rich in potassium and magnesium which are excellent aids for exercise.

Persimmon

Persimmons are very healthy as they have plant compounds that have anti-oxidant and inflammatory qualities. Rich in fiber they are easily digestible aiding weight loss and keeping the gut clean. It's good for the eyes. Rich in Vitamin A. Copper, present in this fruit, helps in proper iron absorption which in turn, aids in the production of red blood cells.It detoxifies the body and liver. Its diuretic in nature and keeps kidneys clean.

Almonds

Almonds are known to give us strength. Rich in healthy fats, antioxidants, vitamins, and minerals. Almonds prevent cell damage and aid in repair.High in Vitamin E, healthy fats, proteins and help to build cell membranes. High in fiber and easily digestible. Very rich in magnesium which can help muscle cramps. Almonds can lower cholesterol levels.

Guava

Guava is high in fiber (very easily digestible). Low in sugar (ideal for diabetics) and has no cholesterol. High vitamin C which improves the overall immune system. Possesses anti-inflammatory properties helping prevent disease. Guava contains strong antioxidant powers, especially red guava. Prevents premature aging.

Strawberries

Strawberries are a rich source of anti-oxidants and fiber. Supports the immune system. Are a good aid to weight loss. Known to have good anti-micro bacterial effects. They also relieve constipation and stress.

Carob

Carob powder is usually used instead of chocolate and is known to be very nutritious as it contains no sodium. Carob powder is high in fiber and is a good source of anti-oxidants. It is also known to provide calcium. Its also known to help relieve diarrhea.

Avocado

Avocados are a rage today. Everyone loves it for its soft texture healthy fats and benefits. Avocado is incredibly nutritious high in fiber, easily digestible and low in sugars. Avocados have healthy fats which are fit for the heart. Rich in Potassium which helps regulate blood pressure. Avocados are high in antioxidants, which help our vision.
It is also mentally uplifting, gives us a fresh feeling and helps the body detoxify.

Mint

Mint is a multi-beneficial ingredient. Its active component is menthol which has anti-septic and antibacterial properties that help relieve indigestion and also soothe an upset stomach.It reduces nasal congestion and helps in oral health. It has tons of anti-inflammatory properties. Its intense aroma can help soothe the mood as well.

Raisin

High in fiber, they help digestion and are known to relieve constipation. Raisins are a good source of iron which helps carry oxygen to the cells of your body. Raisin is calcium-rich and strengthens teeth and bones. Raisins contain tons of antioxidants.

Mango

Mango helps in digestion and is known to boost immunity. Since it has much heat, its known to be good for the eyes and clears the skin. Mango helps weight loss and is filled with anti-oxidants.

Cardamom

Cardamom is a spice which is amazingly beneficial. It is diuretic and lowers blood pressure. It is anti-inflammatory. Very good to improve oral health. Very aromatic and known to fight muscle spasms and ulcers.

Walnuts

Are known as brain nuts, which help nourish the brain tissues and the nerves. Rich in anti-oxidants, decrease inflammation. Extremely good for people with diabetes to regulate sugar. It regulates blood pressure.

Green vegetables are the most healthy ones according to the yogic textbooks. Having greens in the form of juice helps us digest them quicker and absorb the nutrients in the body.

Cilantro

Cilantro is best known to balance sugar levels. It improves vision as it contains Vitamin A. It possesses the right amount of anti-oxidants and helps reduce cholesterol. It supports heart health. Cilantro can help cleanse heavy metals from the body which builds up due to too many artificial additives in food.

Coconut Oil

Is known to lower cholesterol. It aids weight loss. Moisturizes the skin and is known to balance vata or circulation in the body.

Peaches

Peaches are like other fruits high in dietary fiber. Rich in vitamin A and E. Excellent source of potassium, copper, and manganese

Figs

Are very fleshy, tasty and contain minerals and soluble fiber. Figs are rich in minerals such as magnesium, iron and copper. Are rich in vitamin A and K. It's a good source of anti-oxidants. Figs are a great colon cleanser.

Carob Berry

Servings 1

1 cup of frozen organic strawberries
1 ripe frozen banana
1 tablespoon of carob powder
1/2 a cup of raisins soaked overnight
2 teaspoons of Maple syrup (Optional)

Use a Vitamix

Add all the ingredients and add one cup of water.

Blend it for about a minute or until its very creamy and smooth.

Avo Celery Almond

1/2 avacado
1 small cucumber
1/2 a cup of
almonds soaked over-
night
1 cup of celery
Maple syrup(Optional)

Servings 1

Use a Vitamix

Add all the
ingredients and
add half a cup
of water.

Blend it for
about a
minute or until
its very creamy
and smooth.

Blueberry Walnut

1 cup of fresh
blueberries
1 medium frozen
banana
1/2 a cup of walnuts
soaked overnight
1/4 teaspoon of
vanilla bean paste
2 teaspoons of maple
syrup (Optional)
1/2 cup coconut
flakes

Use a Vitamix

Add all the
ingredients and
add one cup
of water.

Blend it for
about a
minute or until
its very creamy
and smooth.

Cantaloupe Avo Almond

1/2 avocado
1 cup of
frozen cantaloupe
chopped.
1 cup of fresh
cantaloupe
chopped
1 cup of spinach
1/2 a cup of
ovenight soaked
almonds
2 teaspoons of
maple syrup (Op-
tional)

Servings 2

Use a Vitamix

Add all the
ingredients and
add half a cup
of water.

Blend it for about a
minute or until its very
creamy and smooth.

Guava Mint

2 ripe medium size guavas
1 ripe frozen banana
1/2 cup of fresh mint leaves
1/2 cup of almonds soaked overnight and peeled
maple syrup (Optional)

Servings 1

Use a Vitamix

Blend the almonds with one cup of water

Now add all the remaining ingredients and blend until creamy and smooth.

Two Layered

PEACH MANGO BANANA
STRAWBERRY

WITH SOAKED
FIGS + RAISINS
SMOOTHIE

Two-layered smoothie

1st layer: Berry-Pineapple-Banana

2nd layer: Avocado-Mint-Celery-Cucumber

No added sugar
(syrup or stevia)

First Layer Ingredients

1/2 cup of strawberry or blueberry
1/2 cup of frozen pineapples
1 banana ripe and frozen.

Second layer ingredients

1 avocado (peeled and sliced)
1/2 cup of almonds soaked overnight
1/2 cup of fresh mint leaves.

Servings 1

Use a Vitamix

1. Add the first layer ingredients in a blender with just half a cup of water and blend it creamy and smooth,then pour it into a jar and make the first layer.
2. Now blend the second layer ingredients with 2 tablespoons of maple syrup and a cup of water until its smooth and creamy.
3. Pour in the same jar that you used to pour the first layer.
4. Gently pour on the top of it slowly making 2 different layers.
5. The thickness of the smoothie will define the 2 layers.

Sometimes the smoothies may have 2 layers on top of each other, and sometimes the smoothie may have layers side by side. A feast for eyes and belly. Yum!

Green Shakti II

1 cup of parsley greens
1/2 cup of celery
1/2 cup of almonds soaked overnight
1 small cucumber
1/2 banana frozen
2 teaspoons of Maple syrup (Optional)

Servings 1

Use a Vitamix

Add all the ingredients and add half a cup of water.

Blend it for about a minute or until its very creamy and smooth.

Persimmon Almond

2 medium sized ripe persimmons chopped
1 frozen banana
1/2 a cup of almonds soaked overnight
1/4 teaspoon of vanilla bean paste
Maple syrup as sweeter (optional)

Servings 2

Use a Vitamix

Add the almonds and half a cup of water and blend it until its very fine.

Now add all the remaining ingredients.

Power blend until its very smooth and creamy texture of the smoothie is attained.

Relish the wonderful persimmon and vanilla flavored smoothie.

Plum Ginger

Use a Vitamix

2 plums peeled and chopped
1 ripe frozen banana
1 inch ginger
1/2 cup water
2 teaspoons
of maple syrup
(Optional)
Servings 2

Add all the ingredients and add half a cup of water.

Blend it for about a minute or until its very creamy and smooth.

Mango Cardamom

1 cup of
ripe mango
chopped
1 ripe   frozen
banana
5 cardamom
pods
2 teaspoons of
maple syrup
(Optional)
Servings 1

Use a Vitamix

Add all the
ingredients and
a cup
of water.

Blend it for
about a
minute or until
its very creamy
and smooth.

Antibiotic

1 cup of mango
1 ripe frozen banana
1/2 teaspoon of turmeric powder
1/2 inch piece of fresh ginger
2 teaspoons of maple syrup (Optional)

Use a Vitamix

Add all the ingredients and add half a cup of water.

Blend it for about a minute or until its very creamy and smooth.

Art of Sprouting

Brown Chick Pea
Soaking Time 10-12 hrs
Sprouting Time 1-2 days

Sprouts are full of life

Sprouting is happiness. Sprouting is a beautiful symptom of life. Once you learn the art of sprouting you will enjoy it so much that you would love to incorporate sprouts in your daily or weekly meals. In our family, we have meal plans where we have sprouted grains and seeds at least twice a week. It is vegan and a wonderful source of vitamins, minerals, proteins in beans, seeds, and grains. When seeds are just about to sprout they are very tender, juicy and nutritious. Sprouts are very easy to digest and full of juice.

Sprouts are very rich in pranic energy infusing us with *prana*, the life energy. They get metabolized very quickly. Sprouting in one sense cooks the seed by freeing up the life energy in the sprout and making it available to us. Sprouting enhances the proteins in the seed by many folds. Sprouting increases phosphorus, calcium, iron, and other useful minerals inside the seed. Sprouting also reduces sugars in the food. Sprouting converts a starchy seed to a nutrient delicious treat.

Sprouts are incredibly healthy. They are the best brain food and are in the mode of goodness. Mode of goodness means healthy, light and easy to digest. Foods that are light , easily digestible and full of energy or *prana* are considered in the mode of goodness in yogic and ayurvedic texts. It not only nourishes the body but calms down the senses and the mind.

Raw sprouts washed thoroughly and sprinkled with a little Himalayan salt taste fantastic. They could also be slightly cooked or sautīed. When they are slightly cooked they digest even more efficiently. Sprouts could be added to salads and even made into burgers. They can be had in a variety of ways. We have added them to salads in a slightly cooked manner.

How to sprout ?

In the pictures following this page the number of hours that a particular grain needs to be soaked is mentioned which can vary anywhere between 8-12 hours depending on the grain. After soaking we need to put them in a 100% cotton muslin cloth to sprout.

Heres the method

After soaking to the respective hours mentioned with pictures in the following pages, drain and wrap them very tight in 100 percent cotton muslin cloth.

Make a knot and place them on top of a glass as shown. Every 10-12 hours pour 1-2 tablespoons of water on top of the muslin cloth if you see them drying.

Using this method there are less chances of rotting as the excess water drains down. During this process make sure you place your sprouts in a clean, dark warm place.

Temperature plays a very important role in the art of sprouting. The thin muslin cloth acts like a soil to the sprouting seeds and 100% germination can take place. I placed my cotton muslin cloths in the oven (turned off of course).

Sprouting is a wonderful art when practicing you experience a deep connection with the food that you put into your body. You will experience fresh, juicy wholesome foods.

Note : Use spring water or filtered water for soaking and sprouting.

Please soak with a covered lid.
For photography purposes we
removed them

Soak Time
Black Eye Beans 8-10 hours
Garbanzo Beans 12-14 hours
Brown Chickpea 10-12 hours
Greengram 8-10 hours
Moth Beans 8-10 hours
Black Beans 10-12 hours

Sprouting Time
Black Eye Beans 1-2 days
Garbanzo Beans 2-3 days
Brown Chickpea 1-2 days
Greengram 1-2 days
Moth Beans 1-2 days
Black Beans 2-3 days

Soak Time
Red Quinoa 8-10 hrs
Mixed Quinoa 8-10 hrs
Fenugreek seeds 8-10 hrs

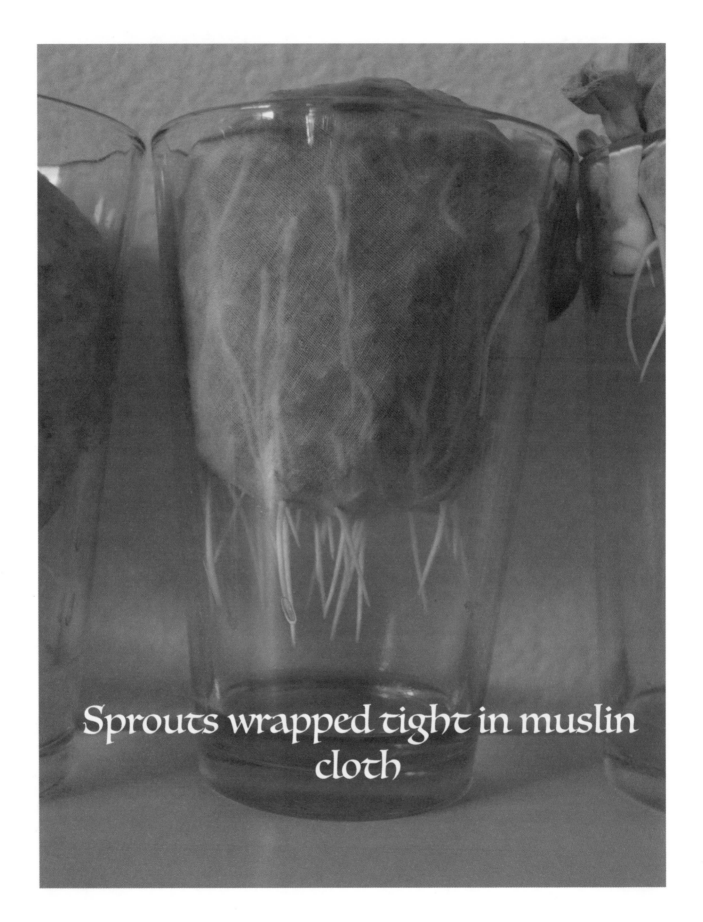

Sprouts wrapped tight in muslin cloth

Green Gram Sprout
Soak Time 8-10 hours
Sprouting Time 1-2 days

Fenugreek Seeds
Soak Time 8-10 Hrs
Sprout Time 1-2 days

Red Quinoa
Soak Time - 8-10 hrs
Sprouting Time 1-2 days

Moth Beans
Soak Time 8-10 hrs
Sprout time 1-2 days

Black Eye Beans
Soak Time 8-10 hrs
Sprout time 1-2 days

Black Beans
Soak Time 8-10 hrs
Sprout Time 2-3 days

Apple Sauce

A healthy choice for anyone, apple sauce is very nutritious and tasty.

SERVES
3

METHOD
BOIL/BLEND

MINUTES
10

DIFFICULTY
3/10

Ingredients

2 honey crisp apples peeled and sliced.

1/2 cup of raisins soaked overnight.

2 cm size of a cinnamon stick.

2 teaspoon of fresh lime juice

Steps

1. In a medium small skillet add 1/2 a cup of water, bring it to boil and add the raisins, sliced apples, cinnamon stick and the lime juice. Close the lid and let it boil and cook for about 3 to 5 minutes on low heat.

2. We are adding the lime juice so that the apples don't turn dark and also maintain their fresh flavors and color.

3. After five minutes open the lid and let it cool down. Now blend the boiled apples with spices in a blender until they turn into a creamy texture as you see in the image.

Rama Raw Salads

Welcome to Rama Raw salads

In general people believe that eating raw is healthy. Going on raw diets are becoming common these days especially vegan plant-based food is gaining popularity. Although it is good to some extent, too much raw food is not good according to ayurveda. You will be surprised to know according to ayurveda raw foods are considered cold, rough and hard to digest. It is said in ayurveda that digestive system works based on the "fire of digestion".

Raw salads are excellent when served with salad dressing which has some form of fat (oils etc) to balance the body fluids and help the raw food digest/cleanse and nourish our body, mind, and soul.

Here at FoodForTheSoul, we will be introducing the concept of eating raw food based on ayurvedic and yogic texts. Great herbs and greens combined with sprouts and salad dressing. These spices, oils, and nuts not only give good taste but they are also good for health.

According to ayurveda, we understand that there is a "fire of digestion" in the stomach which digests all food (This is called *agni* or digestive fire which we have mentioned in the introduction). When the fire is not blazing, there is no hunger, and when the fire is in order, we become hungry. Sometimes when the fire is not functioning well treatment is required. In any case, this fire is considered divine. Vedic mantras also confirm that the Brahman is situated in the form of "fire" within the stomach and is digesting all kinds of foodstuff.

The point is that when we follow scriptures both yogic and ayurvedic, we get the best results in terms of digestion. Food is not just for the body but also for the mind and the soul.

You can have your own combinations of greens as we have shown some combinations here, but the salad dressing that we made is especially nourishing. A combination of slightly cooked sprouts makes it all the more nutritious. We have also added beans in the salads. Although beans are the most underrated they are full of proteins and provide tons of energy.

Servings 3/4

Cooktime 5 mins

Prana Sprouts Salad

Ingredients

2 cups of green gram sprouts

2 cups of turnip greens chopped

1 cup of mixed bell peppers chopped

1 cup of coconut flakes

1 tablespoon of coconut oil

1 teaspoon of mustard seeds

5 slices of fresh Serrano pepper

1 tablespoon of lime juice squeezed fresh

Method

1. Place a medium large skillet on heat. Pour the coconut oil and wait for few seconds for it to heat.

2. Now add the mustard seeds and let them crackle. Then add the sliced Serrano peppers and sautī for 5 seconds.

3. Now add the green gram sprouts, bell peppers and sautī for 2 minutes and then add the turnip greens, salt and sautī for another 1 minute.
Turn off the heat. Squeeze in the fresh lime and toss well. Serve warm.

Beet Tarang Salad Dressing

Ingredients

1 cup of beetroot (peeled, chopped and boiled in 1 cup of water until beet soaks all the water, do not add extra water and strain away the beautiful color and flavor. So use less water and medium heat)

1/2 cup of olive oil.

1 teaspoon of black pepper powder

1 tablespoon of fresh lime squeezed.

1 tablespoon of honey or maple syrup

4 almonds soaked overnight in water. (peel it and just use only the almonds not the water.)

1 cup of water.

Blend all the ingredients until fine and creamy and mix it with desired salad. One good combination is shown in the image.

Moringa

Moringa is a superfood known to be very nutrient. Full of energy it also balances blood sugar levels and can be eaten in a variety of ways. We have Moringa salad dressing, Moringa Chutney and Moringa splatters.

Moringa Salad Dressing

Ingredients

1/2 cup of moringa leaves

2 teaspoons of coconut oil

1/2 cup of mint leaves

1/2 cup of olive oil

1 teaspoon of white and black pepper pods mixed

1 tablespoon of maple syrup

1/4 teaspoon of asafetida powder

1 tablespoon of lime juice

5 almonds soaked overnight

2 teaspoons of coriander seeds

Salt to taste

Steps

1. Place a small skillet on heat and add 2 teaspoons of coconut oil and moringa leaves.

2. Sautī until they turn slightly darker. Should take about 3-4 minutes. Turn off the heat add the asafetida and mint leaves. Wait for it to cool down.

3. Now put these seasoned leaves in a blender and add all the remaining ingredients with a cup of water and blend them in a couple of intervals until very fine and creamy.

4. Mix with your desired combination of salad mix as shown in the image.

SERVES
2

METHOD
BOIL ,SAUTE

MINUTES
10

DIFFICULTY
5/10

Fenugreek Sprouts Spice Balls

Ingredients

1 cup of sprouted fenugreek seeds
2 medium sized red potatoes boiled, peeled and mashed
1/2 cup of purple cabbage chopped very small.
1/2 cup of green bell pepper chopped small cubes.
1 tablespoon coconut oil
1 teaspoon cumin seeds
1/4 teaspoon of nutmeg powder
1/2 teaspoon white pepper powder
1/2 teaspoon red chili powder
1 cup of fresh cilantro chopped

1 tablespoon lime juice freshly squeezed

1 tablespoon of lime juice squeezed fresh

Steps

1. Place a medium sized skillet on heat. Pour in the coconut oil and wait for few seconds for the oil to be well heated.

2. Add the cumin seeds and wait for 5 seconds,then add the fenugreek sprouts and saute on medium heat for about 3 minutes.

3. Now lower the heat and continue tossing for about another 3 minutes.

 4. Now add the chopped bell peppers, cabbage, black pepper powder, quarter teaspoon of nutmeg powder and salt.

5. Mix and toss well for 5 seconds and then add the mashed potatoes and mix well making sure all the veggies and sprouts are well mixed into the mashed potatoes.

6. Turn off the heat. Wait for few minutes until it's semi cooled. Add the fresh cilantro and lime juice and make small balls of 3 cm diameter.

Serve it warm as side dish for lunch or dinner. If you like savory for breakfast you can have it with morning tea as well.

Avocado Parsley Dressing

SERVES
4

METHOD
BLEND

MINUTES
10

DIFFICULTY
3/10

Ingredients

Ingredients: Here in the image I have all organic carrots (red, yellow, orange &white), lettuce, bell peppers, avocados & celery. You can make a combination of salads and greens of your choice .

5-6 nos almonds

1/2 avocado

1 cup of chopped parsley

1 inch piece of ginger

3 tablespoon olive oil

2 tablespoon of raw honey

2 tsp black pepper powder

1 fresh lime squeezed

1 cup of water and Himalayan pink salt as needed.

Steps

1. Add all ingredients into a blender
2. Blend for a minute and wait for few seconds and blend again until you get a creamy texture.
3. Mix it with the colorful salad and nourish your soul.

One way to keep ourselves light
is by having soups regularly.
Soups are very easy on the body.

The need to breakdown the food
is avoided as the boiled and
blended vegetables are easily
assimilated in the body.

There are some plants which are
better than the others in terms
of metabolism and medicinal
properties.

Here we are providing soups
with both nutritional and
medicinal value. What goes into
the soups is the vegetables and
some spicing. Spicing is very
important as they are essential
digestive aids.
They provide flavor as well.

Rejuvenating Soups

Moringa Moong Bean Soup

SERVES
2

METHOD
BOIL/BLEND

MINUTES
20

DIFFICULTY
4/10

Ingredients

3/4 cup of fresh Moringa leaves

1 cup of yellow moong beans triple washed and soaked for an hour

Half a cup of shredded coconut

1 teaspoon of mixed red, white, black pepper pods

1 teaspoon of cumin seeds

Dash of lime juice

Steps

1. Boil the moong beans in 4 cups for water until soft and tender.

2. In a blender grind the moringa leaves, pepper pods, cumin seeds, and shredded coconut until fine paste-like texture with an added cup of water.

3. After the moong beans are well cooked, add this blended mixture to it, add salt and let it simmer for another 5 minutes on low heat.

Turn off the heat garnish with few fresh Moringa leaves, shredded coconut, and dash of lime. Serve hot.

Brocoli Soup

Ingredients

2 cups of broccoli riced.

2 cups of spinach blended into fine puree

2 cups of coconut milk

1 tablespoon of corn starch mixed in 4 tablespoons of water

1/2 a teaspoon black pepper powder

1 tablespoon coconut oil

SERVES 2	METHOD BLEND,BOIL	MINUTES 10	DIFFICULTY 3/10

Steps

1. Take a medium skillet. Pour in the coconut oil and the black pepper powder.

2. Now pour the spinach puree and sautī for 3 minutes.

3. Add a cup of water and bring it to boil.

4. Add the riced broccoli, coconut milk, corn starch and salt.

5. Stir well and bring it to boil, then let it simmer on low heat for about 5 minutes

6. Turn off the heat serve hot with a slice of lime.

Ingredients

1/2 a cup of fresh green beans chopped

1/2a cup of bell peppers chopped

1/2 a cup of carrots chopped

1/2 a cup of celery chopped

1/2 a cup of broccoli chopped

3 ripe tomatoes chopped

Rice noodles or noodles of your own choice

2 tablespoons of sesame oil

1/2 inch ginger minced fine

5 fresh basil leaves

2 teaspoon of Italian seasoning

1/2 teaspoon of black pepper powder

Noodle Soup

SERVES
3

METHOD
SAUTE,BOIL

MINUTES
20

DIFFICULTY
5/10

Steps

1. Take a large skillet and place it on heat. Add 2 tablespoons of   sesame oil.

2. Wait for 10 to 15 seconds for the oil to be well heated. Now add the chopped tomatoes. Increase the heat and sautī the tomatoes until entirely tender and mushy releasing all its flavor.

3. Reduce the heat to medium, and you may close the lid of the skillet for the tomatoes to cook nice and tender.

4. After the tomatoes are wholly mushy and tender, now it's time to add 8 cups of water and bring it to boil.

5. Add about two or three handfuls of rice noodles or noodles of your choice.

Based on your desire you could add plenty of noodles to the soup or little. In this recipe, I have used more noodles because my family loves to have a lot of noodles with veggies and the water of the soup.

6. Now let the noodles cook in this tomato flavored water.

7. At this time add all the vegetables, salt to taste and ginger.

8. Turn off the heat after the noodles are cooked. You don't want the veggies to be overcooked or extremely tender.

9. We want the vegetables to infuse all the excellent flavor and   slightly tender but crunchy enough. Add fresh basil and the Italian seasoning and close the lid for about another 3 minutes.

This is an excellent one pot dish to be served as dinner.

SERVES 3	**METHOD** SAUTE,BOIL BLEND	**MINUTES** 10	**DIFFICULTY** 2/10

Butternut Squash Soup

Ingredients

2 cups of chopped butternut squash

1/2 cup of cabbage chopped

2 ripe tomatoes chopped

1-inch piece of ginger

1/2 teaspoon of black pepper powder

1 Tablespoon of coconut oil

5 to 8 fresh basil leaves

1/2 a teaspoon of turmeric powder

Steps

1. Please a large skillet on heat. Now pour the coconut oil and let it heat up for 10-15 seconds and then add the chopped cabbage and tomatoes first.

2. Sautī for about five minutes then add the butternut squash.

3. Increase the heat from medium to high and stirring   continuously let it cook for about 2 to 3 minutes then add the ginger, black pepper powder, and the basil leaves.

4. Stir well and then add 2 cups of water. Close the lid and let it simmer for about 8 to 10 minutes or until the butternut squash is soft and tender. Open the lid and turn off the heat.

5. Now use a hand blender placing it in the pot, blend the squash with the other veggies into a fine paste.

6. Now add another cup of water if needed and let it simmer for about another five minutes.

7. Garnish with chopped fresh basil leaves and a creamy butternut squash soup is ready.

SERVES
2

METHOD
BOIL

MINUTES
25

DIFFICULTY
3/10

Barley Soup

Barley detoxes and balances most of our health parameters.

Ingredients

1 cup of barely

1 cup of broccoli chopped into small size

1 cup of celery chopped

1/2 cup of carrots shredded.

1/2 cup of red and yellow bell peppers chopped.

1/2 teaspoon of black pepper powder.

2 teaspoons of coconut oil

Steps

1. Wash and soak barley for couple

of hours then boil it in extra 5 cups of water.

2. Close the lid and let it simmer on medium heat for

about 15 minutes

2. Check if the barley grain is cooked and tender.

3. Then add the spices, salt and veggies. Turn off the heat.

4. Close lid for 5 minutes. Open the lid, serve it hot with

two teaspoons of coconut oil and garnished with cilantro.

Bottlegourd Soup

Bottlegourd can be cooked in all conditions, whether one is sick or dieting. It's excellent for the body and mind.

SERVES
2

METHOD
BLEND

MINUTES
10

DIFFICULTY
2/10

Ingredients

3 cups of bottle guard peeled and chopped

1 inch piece ginger chopped

1/2 teaspoon of white pepper powder

1/2 cup of fresh cilantro chopped

1 teaspoon of cornstarch

1 cup of coconut milk

2 teaspoons of fresh lime juice

2 teaspoons of coconut oil

Steps

1. Bring two cups of water to boil and add the chopped bottle gourd, ginger and let it simmer for about 5 minutes with closed lid. (do not overcook, you need to have the nice light green color and the fresh flavor of bottle gourd)

2. Now open the lid and add corn starch mixed with three teaspoons of water and coconut milk. Then use the hand blender. Place in the center of the pot and blend until nice and creamy soup.

3. The texture is seen with no pieces of the bottle guard is visible.

4. Now bring to boil once more, add pepper and serve hot with drizzled white pepper powder, cilantro, and fresh lime squeezed. Very healthy and healing soup. Always cook bottle guard very simple. Do not mix with many vegetables and too many spices. It minimizes the medicinal effect of the soup.

Sprout Soup

A sprout soup gives you the goodness of both sprouts and a soup

SERVES
4

METHOD
SAUTE,BOIL

MINUTES
10

DIFFICULTY
6/10

Ingredients

3 cups of green gram sprout

(Follow the sprouting instructions in the section, art of sprouting

page number 72)

3 ripe tomatoes

2 tablespoon of dried mint leaves (pudina)

1 inch ginger

1 teaspoon of black and white peppers

2 tablespoons of coconut oil

1 cup of fresh cilantro chopped

1/2 teaspoon of turmeric

Steps

1. In a blender add the chopped tomatoes, mint, black pepper and turmeric.
Blend it until it's a very fine puree.

2. Now place a medium, large skillet on heat and pour the coconut oil into it and the puree that you just made fresh.

3. Close the lid and let it cook on medium heat for about 5-8 minutes. Open the lid and check if the puree has turned dark red and has absorbed all the flavors.

4. Now add the sprouts and salt to taste, toss well upside down making sure that the sprouts are well coated with the puree. Add salt and mix well and close the lid for about another 5   minutes on low heat.

5. Open the lid and add 4 cups of water, as much as the water soaks the sprouts and 1 cm above the sprout level. Let it come to boil and simmer for about 3 minutes and turn off the heat, garnish with fresh cilantro and serve hot.

Mukunda Minestrone Soup

SERVES
4

METHOD
SAUTE, BOIL,

MINUTES
25

DIFFICULTY
5/10

Ingredients

5 ripe tomatoes, sliced in to 4 pieces.

2 tablespoons olive oil.

1 cup of overnight soaked and boiled soft tri color beans. (Pinto beans, kidney beans, black beans)

1 cup of elbow pasta or if you like more pasta add a 1/2 cup more. (To make it gluten free, use gluten free pasta)

1/2 a cup carrots chopped.

1 cup zucchini chopped.

1/2 a cup green bell peppers chopped.

1/2 teaspoon black pepper powder.

1 teaspoon paprika powder.

1 1/2 teaspoon Italian seasoning.

1/2 teaspoon asafetida

5 to 8 fresh basil leaves.

Steps

1. Take a large skillet and place it on medium heat, pour the olive oil. Wait for 3 minutes then add asafetida and sliced tomatoes and cook for 10 minutes with closed lid.

2. After the tomatoes are tender and juicy, add 2 cups of water and using a hand blender, blend the tomatoes into a nice fine sauce. Now add six more cups of water and bring it to boil.

3. Then add the elbow pasta. After the pasta is halfway cooked, add all the chopped vegetables, close the lid and simmer it on medium heat. After 5-8 mins (check if the vegetables are cooked) add the tri-color pre-boiled beans and let it boil on medium heat for five more minutes, in between add all the spices and salt.

5. At this point add more water if needed. Now bring it to one final boil and turn off the heat with an open lid. (if you close the lid, the sauce might overflow from the cooking pot and spill on your cooktop). Garnish with fresh basil leaves. Serve hot.

Pumpkin Soup

SERVES
3

METHOD
BOIL,BLEND

MINUTES
20

DIFFICULTY
5/10

Ingredients

3 cups of pumpkin peeled and chopped

Pumpkin seeds saved from the fresh pumpkin
washed and dried on a washcloth

1/2 teaspoon of black pepper powder

2 tablespoon of coconut oil

1/2 cup coconut milk

1/2 slice of lime juice

1/2 cup fresh parsley chopped

1/2 teaspoon of Italian seasoning

1. Place a medium sized skillet on heat. Pour in the coconut oil. Now add the chopped pumpkin and salt to taste. Sautī for about 5 to 8 minutes on medium heat. Close lid for another two minutes.

2. Open the lid, now Add 4 cups of water and bring it to boil. Close the lid again and let it simmer for about another 5 to 8 minutes on medium low heat.

3. Open the lid, check if the pumpkin is cooked and tender, then use a hand blender put it in the center and blend the pumpkin into a very fine puree. If you wish to have a nice and thick creamy soup leave it the same way and let it simmer for another five minutes. And if you want to dilute it further, this is the time to add another cup or 2 cups of water, add salt and stir well.

4. Add the spices and half a cup of coconut milk. Serve hot with freshly squeezed lemon/ lime juice on top. Also add the roasted pumpkin seeds.

5. After the pumpkin seeds are washed and dried.

6. Place a flat pan on heat add 1 teaspoon of coconut oil and add all the pumpkin seeds and roast them until they turn slightly golden brown looking crispy.

7. Serve the pumpkin seeds on the side of the soup and garnish some of it on the top of the soup along with fresh parsley chopped.

Baking

Over Frying

Raw Banana

Plantain

Brahmanda Banana/Plantain

SERVES
4

METHOD
BAKE

MINUTES
45

DIFFICULTY
4/10

Ingredients

5 raw bananas/plantain peeled and sliced as shown in the image

2 teaspoons of paprika

1 teaspoon of black pepper powder

2 tablespoons of coconut oil

½ teaspoon of cayenne pepper powder (optional)

1 cup of rice flour

½ cup of cornstarch

Steps

1. In a large mixing bowl add the raw bananas, salt and spices mix well let them sit for about 10 to 15 minutes.

2. Now add all of the remaining ingredients rice flour and corn starch and toss well upside down making sure every slice is coated with flour, spices, and oil.

3. Let it sit for another five minutes. Place each slice individually at some distance from each other on a baking tray.

4. Bake it in the oven at the 380° F for about 20 - 25 minutes/ until the edges are golden brown and look crispy on the outside and ready cooked on the inside. The   beautiful yummy Brahma baked, raw banana is ready.

Breadfruit Baked

SERVES
3

METHOD
BAKE

MINUTES
40

DIFFICULTY
4/10

Ingredients

1 breadfruit raw (washed and sliced 1 cm thickness
removing the middle part as shown in the image)
1 teaspoon of black pepper powder
1 1/2 teaspoon of cumin powder
1/2 teaspoon of paprika
1 tablespoon of olive oil
1 tablespoon of coconut oil
1/2 teaspoon of asafetida

Steps

1. Put all the sliced breadfruit in a large bowl add the salt
and spices and keep it inside with a closed lid for about 10
minutes.
2. Then open the lid and add the olive oil, coconut oil and toss
well.
3. At this time add the rice flour by sprinkling one teaspoon
or 2 teaspoons of water allowing the rice to be well mixed
with the spices and oil to be well coated on each slice of the
breadfruit.
4. After mixing well preheat the oven.
5. In a large flat baking tray place individual slices with the
distance not sticking to each other bake at 380° F for about
20 minutes until the edges turn golden brown as seen in the
image.

Quinoa Burger

A supergrain burger

SERVES
5

METHOD
BAKE

MINUTES
30

DIFFICULTY
6/10

Ingredients

2 cups of quinoa boiled in 3 cups of water until it absorbs all the water. It should be semi-cooked

2 cups of mashed potato

1 cup of rice flour

1 teaspoon of white pepper powder

1 cup of cilantro chopped

3 tablespoons of olive oil

1/2 a cup of shredded carrot

1/2 a teaspoon of minced jalapeno 1/2 a teaspoon of nutmeg powder

1 cup of olive oil

Method

1. Combine all the ingredients in a large mixing bowl. Add salt to it, mix well make it into a semi-soft dough. Make 8-10 equal sizes of balls.

2. Press it making it 1 cm thick and about 2 inches diameter in size. Place it on parchment sheet on a baking tray. Bake at 380° F for about 15 -20 minutes or till the edges turn crispy.

3. Serve it hot with carrot bell chutney or turn it into a desired burger with bread lettuce and tomato.

SERVES
3

METHOD
BAKE

MINUTES
10

DIFFICULTY
3/10

Asparagus Baked

Ingredients

1 lb of asparagus

1 tablespoon of rice flour

1/2 a tablespoon of cornstarch

2 tablespoons of olive oil

1 teaspoon of Italian seasoning

1/2 a teaspoon of black pepper powder

Salt to taste

1 tablespoon of coconut flakes

Steps

1. In a small bowl add all the spices flour, oil, and salt.

2. Take a small whisker and whisk for 3-5 minutes. Now chop off about 1 inch of asparagus from the bottom.

3. Now place them on the baking sheet, pour the mixture and toss them well upside down with your hands making sure that all the   asparagus is well coated with the seasoning.

4. You could also use a brush and brush them well with the seasoning. Bake it in the oven at 480º F about 3-5 minutes. Add coconut flakes in the end.

Steps

1. Add all the chopped zucchini to a large mixing bowl

2. In a blender blend all the spices,oil, soaked rice(completely strained) with 1/2 a cup of water. Do not blend the sesame seeds.

 2. Mix the zucchini with all the blended spices, salt and sesame seeds

3. Preheat the oven on 380º F.

4. On a baking tray place the parchment sheet and place each zucchini slice slightly apart from each other. Bake for about 15 minutes. Then broil for about 3-5 minutes/ until edges turn brown and crispy outside.

5. Take the tray out and place all the baked zucchini in a tray and garnish with freshly chopped cilantro and dry coconut powder.

Baked Zucchini Crisp

SERVES 4	**METHOD** BAKE	**MINUTES** 30	**DIFFICULTY** 5/10

Ingredients

3 medium size the zucchini sliced long and thick as shown in the image.

1/2 a cup of basmati rice soaked for 3 hours

1/2 a cup of cornstarch

1teaspoon whole black pepper

½ teaspoon nutmeg powder

2 teaspoon of whole coriander

1 tablespoon of coconut oil.

½ a cup of white sesame seeds

Baked Samosa

SERVES
6

METHOD
BOIL, BAKE

MINUTES
50

DIFFICULTY
8/10

A healthy way to eat the samosas. Baked with herbs and spices and a very little bit of olive oil. Crispy on the outer tasty stuffing on the inside is a yummy snack for a morning tea time or an evening tea time.

Ingredients

For the dough

3 cups of all-purpose flour

½ cup of flex flour

2 teaspoons of carom seeds

1 teaspoon of baking powder

2 tablespoons of olive oil

Salt to taste

For the filling

4 medium sized golden potatoes boiled, peeled and mashed.

½ a teaspoon of black pepper powder

½ teaspoon of nutmeg powder

¼ teaspoon of cinnamon powder

1 teaspoon of coriander seeds powder

½ teaspoon of cardamom powder

½ a cup of chopped cilantro.

1 lime juice squeezed

1/2 a teaspoon of turmeric powder

1 teaspoon of cumin seeds

1 tablespoon of coconut oil

Steps

First to prepare the filling.

1. Place a medium-sized skillet on medium heat. Pour the coconut oil. Once the oil is heated well add cumin seeds, asafetida and then toss all the mashed potato into it and mix well upside down making sure it's cooked well but not burnt.

Now add the salt and all the spices to it. Mix well. Turn off the heat and add the fresh cilantro and the lime juice, mix well and keep aside.

Now prepare the dough

1. Take a medium-large mixing bowl. Add all-purpose flour and the flax meal, baking powder spices, and herbs.

Mix well making sure the spices salt and baking soda are evenly mixed all over the flour.

2. Now add the olive oil and using both your hands keep rubbing the flour in between your palms Making sure the oil is mixed all over the flour.

3. Now take some lukewarm water and keep adding slowly to the flour and knead into a nice dough like the consistency that of any pizza base dough or any flat bread dough (slightly firm but good enough to roll into thin flat breads). Let it sit for 10-15 minutes with closed lid.

4. Now make 10-15 equal size balls of the dough. Then using a rolling pin roll into a 5-inch diameter flat bread. Cut into half and put one spoon of stuffing and fold into triangles as shown in the image.

5. Then place all the folded triangle samosas in a baking tray. Preheat the oven at 380° F and bake for 20 minutes or until edges turn golden brown and crispy.

Hot Somasas ready. Serve with tangy Date tamarind chutney. (@ Chakra chutney corner)

Baked
Falafel

Baked Falafel

Ingredients

SERVES
6

3 cups of overnight soaked garbanzo beans

2 cup of fresh parsley chopped

1 inch piece of ginger

11/2 teaspoon of black pepper powder

1/2 a cup of olive oil

1 teaspoon of baking powder

1 cup of mint leaves

Juice of 1 squeezed lime

METHOD
BAKE

Steps

1. Using a food processor add the garbanzo beans olive oil, ginger and process it until a fine paste.

2. Now add all the remaining ingredients and process it until nice and smooth texture.

MINUTES
40

3. Take a large baking tray make them into flat burgers or roll them into small balls bake it in the oven at 380° F for about 20 minutes, or the edges turn golden brown.

4. In the image, I have made them flat because I also like using falafel into the sandwiches or flat breads or cut them and added to the salad.

DIFFICULTY
5/10

5. For making a dip to go with falafel go to the recipe of Tomato Tahini in the chakra chutney corner.

Chakra
Chutney Corner

Mint Almond Chutney

SERVES
5

METHOD
BLEND

MINUTES
10

DIFFICULTY
1/10

Ingredients

2 cups of fresh mint leaves

1/2 cup of almonds

1 small Serrano pepper

1/2 inch ginger

1 teaspoon maple syrup

1/2 teaspoon cumin seeds

1 tablespoon of fresh lime juice.

Steps

1. Blend all the ingredients in a blender with one cup of water (add salt to taste) until fine creamy texture.

Purple Chutney

SERVES
4

METHOD
BLEND

MINUTES
10

DIFFICULTY
2/10

Ingredients

1 cup of chopped purple cabbage.

2 cups of freshly grated coconut.

1/2 inch piece of Ginger & Black pepper

1 teaspoon asafetida.

1/2 teaspoon suger.

1/2 of cup of water.

salt to taste

Steps

Put all the ingredients in a blender and blend it smooth. Add some water if needed. (great combination with dosas, appams and idlis)

Peanut cilantro chutney

SERVES
4

METHOD
BLEND

MINUTES
15

DIFFICULTY
4/10

Ingredients

1 tablespoon coconut oil

1/2 a cup of peanuts

1 cup of fresh cilantro

1/2 teaspoon cumin seeds

1/2 teaspoon blackpepper pods

3-4 slices of serrano peppers

1 tablespoon of lime juice

Steps

1. Place a small skillet on heat. Pour the coconut oil into it. Toss the peanuts and cumin seeds. Sautī for a few seconds until the peanuts turn dark brown and look crispy.

2. Turn off the heat, add salt and cilantro, 1 tablespoon of lime juice.

3. Let it semi cool and blend it with a cup of water.

SERVES
4

METHOD
BLEND

MINUTES
10

DIFFICULTY
3/10

Cilantro Mustard Dip

Something very tasty, tangy and healthy

Ingredients

1 cup of fresh cilantro chopped

1/2 cup almonds

1 teaspoon of black mustard seeds

1/2-inch piece of ginger

1 teaspoon of black pepper pods

1 tablespoon of fresh lime juice squeezed

1 tablespoon of honey or maple syrup

Steps

1. Toss and all the ingredients of cilantro dip in a blender and add 1 cup of water and salt and blend until fine creamy texture.

2. Add a little water if you think it is thick and pour it into a small bowl to be served with mini burgers.

Chinese Okra Skin Chutney

SERVES
8

METHOD
BLEND

MINUTES
20

DIFFICULTY
7/10

Ingredients

Peels of 2 Chinese okra

5-8 slices of Serrano pepper

1 cm of cinnamon bark

1 inch piece of ginger

2 tablespoons of lime juice

2 tablespoons of coconut oil

1/2 a teaspoon of mustard seeds

1/2 a teaspoon of cumin seeds

1/2 a teaspoon of asafetida

1 cup of cilantro

1/2 a teaspoon turmeric powder

1/2 a cup of almonds

2 teaspoons of coriander seeds

Steps

1. Place a medium skillet on heat and pour the coconut oil into it and let it heat for 10-15 secs.

2. Toss in the mustard cumin seeds followed by asafetida. Add the Serrano peppers, cinnamon bark and sautī it for another 5-8   seconds.

3. Toss in the peels of Chinese okra and mix well upside down,   ensure that they are well seasoned. Cook for about 5-8 minutes until the peels look dark green.

4. Add salt and turmeric. Turn off the heat and let it cool down for about 10 minutes.

5. Add the lime juice, almonds, cilantro, salt and a cup of water.

Now pour everything into a blender and blend, add extra water if needed. Blend

Tomato
Tahini
cumin, coriander seeds, black

Tomato Tahini

SERVES
2

METHOD
BLEND

MINUTES
10

DIFFICULTY
2/10

Ingredients

1 cup of white sesame seeds

2 cups of ripe tomatoes chopped

1 teaspoon cumin seeds

2 teaspoon of coriander seeds

1 teaspoon white pepper pods

1 tablespoon sesame oil

1 inch piece ginger

1/2 a cup of fresh cilantro chopped

Steps

1. Place a medium skillet on heat. Pour the sesame oil and let it heat for a few seconds. Add cumin seeds and wait until they crackle.

2. Then add coriander seeds, white pepper pods, and sesame seeds. Reduce the heat to low and sautī the spices for 10-15 seconds.

3. Now add the chopped tomatoes and salt. Sautī well until the tomatoes are tender and juicy. Close the lid and let it cook for 5 minutes on medium heat. Turn off the heat and let it semi-cool down.

4. Then blend it very fine by adding half a cup of water. Garnish with cilantro, Tomato slices, roasted sesame seeds. Serve with phal Falafel or any splatters or flat breads.

Date Tamarind Chutney

SERVES
10

METHOD
BOIL, BLEND

MINUTES
45

DIFFICULTY
5/10

Ingredients

1 cup of dates soaked overnight (unseeded)

1/2 cup of raisins soaked overnight

1/2 a cup of tamarind pulp

1 tablespoon of coriander seeds

2 teaspoons of fennel seeds

1 teaspoon of black salt

1/4 teaspoon of cinnamon powder

1/2 teaspoon of cayenne pepper

1/2 teaspoon of white pepper powder

Steps

1. Blend the soaked dates, raisins, tamarind with two cups of water until smooth. Pour it into a skillet and bring it to boil. Lower the heat and let it simmer for about 15 mins on low heat.

2. Dry roast all the spices individually for about 10 seconds each. Use a spice grinder and grind all the spices together into a fine powder.

3. After the chutney is simmered and thicker in texture add the spices and stir well.

4. Add salt as needed. Date Tamarind Chutney is ready. Great for samosas, baked burgers and splatters.

Pumpkin Chutney

SERVES
4

METHOD
BLEND

MINUTES
25

DIFFICULTY
5/10

Ingredients

10 -12 large cubes of yellow pumpkin

1/2 inch piece of ginger

2 teaspoon mustard seeds.

2 teaspoon coriander seeds.

1/2 teaspoon asafetida.

1/2 teaspoon black pepper powder.

1/2 teaspoon cayenne pepper (optional)

1 tablespoon coconut oil for cooking.

1 tablespoon of almond flour.

Steps

1. In a medium skillet add 1 tbsp coconut oil and place it on heat for 20 seconds. Now add all the spices and sautī well for 3 to 4 minutes (until you hear the mustard seeds crackle).

2. Then add the chopped tomatoes,salt and pumpkin and mix well. After 3 minutes add 1 cup of water and salt and close the lid, let it cook for 10 minutes (until pumpkin and tomatoes are soft and tender).

3. Wait until semi-cool. Then blend it by adding lime juice and almond flour until a fine paste. Add water if needed. Goes well with idli.

Kriyas are major cleansing
processes mentioned in the yogic texts.
After cleansing one needs to eat simple
khichris to build up mucus lining   and
digestion. Khichris digest faster and
magnifies the effect of cleansing.

After Kriya Khichri

Rice Moong Bean Khichri

The simplest of all khichris

SERVES
4

METHOD
BOIL

MINUTES
30

DIFFICULTY
5/10

Ingredients

1 cup of basmati rice

1 1/2 cup of moong beans yellow

1/2 teaspoon turmeric powder

1 tablespoon of Coconut oil (Vegan) or Ghee (clarified Butter)

Steps

There are Two ways to make this khichri.

1. One is to put all the ingredients in an instant pot or pressure cooker and cook it very soft with added salt and Coconut oil (Vegan) or Ghee. (Clarified Butter)

2. And the other procedure is to cook with open lid. Wash the rice and the mung beans separately, now cook the rice like you cook regular basmati rice with 1:2 cups of water until the rice cooks firm.

Simultaneously in another pot, boiling the moong beans (in three times its volume in water) and then cooking it with an extra 4 cups of water until very soft and tender.

Now mix the cooked moong beans into the rice pot and gently mix not breaking the basmati rice. Now keep the pot on medium heat and add turmeric powder and salt to taste. Close the lid and let it simmer for about 10 minutes. Open the lid and add some coconut oil (vegan)/ clarified butter and garnish with fresh cilantro to this and your yogic Kichiri is ready.

Quinoa Khichri

SERVES
4

METHOD
BOIL

MINUTES
30

DIFFICULTY
5/10

Ingredients

1 cup of Quinoa

1 1/2 cup of moong beans yellow

1/2 teaspoon turmeric powder

1 tablespoon of Coconut oil(Vegan)or Ghee (clarified Butter)

1 cup cilantro

Steps

There are Two ways to make this khichri.

1. One is to put all the ingredients in an instant pot or pressure cooker and cook it very soft with added salt and Coconut oil(Vegan)or Ghee (clarified Butter)

2. And the other procedure is to cook with open lid. Wash the quinoa and the moong beans separately, now cook the quinoa like you cook regular quinoa with 1: 2 cups of water until the quinoa cooks firm.

Simultaneously in another pot, boiling the moong beans (in three times its volume in water) and then cooking it with an extra 4 cups of water until very soft and tender.

Now mix the cooked moong beans into the quinoa pot and gently mix. Now keep the pot on medium heat and add turmeric powder and salt to taste. Close the lid let it simmer for about 10 minutes. Open the lid and add some coconut oil(Vegan)/clarified butter and garnish with riced brocolli and shredded carrots, colored bell peppers(Optional) fresh cilantro to this and your yogic Kichiri is ready.

Chayote Kale khichri

SERVES
4

METHOD
BOIL

MINUTES
35

DIFFICULTY
6/10

Ingredients

1 cup of chopped chayote

2 cup of chopped baby kale leaves

1 cup of ripe tomatoes chopped

1 cup of green gram split

1 cup of basmati rice

1 teaspoon cumin seeds

1 teaspoon turmeric powder

1 inch of ginger grated

1/2 cup of shredded carrot

2 tablespoon of coconut oil

1 teaspoon of white pepper powder.

2 inch bar of cinnamon stick

Fresh lime slices to garnish

Ingredients

1. In a medium bowl put the rice, the green gram splits together and washed it three times and let it soak for at least 30 minutes.

2. Now place a cooking pot on heat. Pour the coconut oil and let it heat for about a minute.

3. Add cumin seeds grated ginger, cinnamon bark, turmeric and sautī for about 3 to 5 seconds, add in the washed rice and green gram by straining away the excess water. Keep stirring on high heat for about 3 minutes.

4. Now add 6 cups of water and let it boil on medium heat until the rice and split green gram are half cooked with a closed lid. Now add the chopped chayote, shredded carrots and tomatoes to the boiling pot and cook with closed lid for another 10 minutes.

5. Now add the freshly chopped kale leaves and the wonderful chayote Kale Kichiri is ready.

Garnish with white pepper powder and fresh lime squeezed on the top. Serve hot!

Radiant

Rice

SERVES 2	**METHOD** BOIL	**MINUTES** 40	**DIFFICULTY** 6/10

Blueberry Sweet Rice

Ingredients

½ a cup of black rice or forbidden rice

1 cup of ripe blueberries

½ a cup of maple syrup

1 cup of coconut milk

1/4 teaspoon of vanilla bean paste/ 1 teaspoon of vanilla essence

Steps

1. Wash the forbidden rice and boil it in a medium skillet with 2 cups of water for 20 minutes or until the water is almost dried and rice is very tender.

2. Now blend the blueberries in a blender and pour the fresh blueberry puree into the rice pot.

3. Leave it on medium flame and let it cook until the rice absorbs the fresh juice of the blueberries.

4. When it turns thick and creamy, turn off the heat.

5. Wait until the rice cools down to room temperature and then add the maple syrup,vanilla bean paste and the coconut milk. Mix thoroughly.

The vegan blueberry sweet rice is ready.

 SERVES 3	 METHOD SAUTE	 MINUTES 15	 DIFFICULTY 3/10

Broccoli Rice

Ingredients

2 cups of fine chopped broccoli

1 1/2 cup of cooked cooled basmati rice

1 tablespoon of ghee or coconut oil

1/2 a teaspoon of turmeric powder

1/4 teaspoon of paprika

Steps

1. Take a medium sized skillet. Place it on heat and add coconut oil (vegan) or ghee

2. Toss in the chopped broccoli and add the spices and salt to taste. Sautī for about three minutes on medium heat.

3. Toss in the cooked rice and mix well on medium heat for about another three minutes. The simple broccoli rice is ready.

SERVES
4

METHOD
INSTANT POT

MINUTES
30

DIFFICULTY
6/10

Purple Pulav

Ingredients

1 1/2 cups of purple cabbage finally chopped

2 cups of basmati Rice washed and strained

1/2 a cup of green beans chopped

1 inch of ginger grated fine

2 tablespoons of coconut oil(vegan) / ghee (clarified butter)

1 teaspoon nutmeg powder

1/2 teaspoon cinnamon powder

1/2 teaspoon black pepper powder

1 cup cilantro chopped

4 bay leaves

1 tomato chopped

1 green bell pepper chopped

Steps

First, in a blender add ginger,black pepper powder and handful of cabbage. Blend it into a fine paste. This recipe comes out to be perfect using an instant pot or a pressure cooker.

Using a 5 L pressure cooker,

1. Place it on medium heat and add coconut oil, after 10 to 15 seconds add cumin seeds. Then add the bay leaves and then add the strained basmati rice and roast it on high heat for about 3 minutes. We are roasting the rice in the seasoning of cumin and bay leaves for them to have a pleasant aroma and you have a very lovely Pulav which isn't sticking together.

2. After roasting the rice in the coconut oil evenly, put in the ginger cabbage paste that you made and stir it well. Now add the salt and all the vegetables and remaining spices and once again mix well very gently so that you don't break the raw rice (to have an excellent long grain basmati rice in the end) quickly pour in the 3 1/2 cups of boiling water.

4. Gently stir one more time and close the lid. After one whistle turn off the cooker/instant pot. If you are cooking in an open container, let it cook on medium heat for 10- 15 minutes or until all the water is absorbed then turn off the heat and let it sit for another 15 minutes.

Wild Rice Stirfry

Wild rice although not technically rice is special and considered very nutrient

SERVES
2

METHOD
SAUTE

MINUTES
15

DIFFICULTY
5/10

Ingredients

1 cup of mixed wild rice boiled and cooled

1 cup of semi ripe plantain /raw plantain sliced oval (which means sliced in cross ways making oval shapes instead of circles.

1 cup of Chinese long beans

1/2 cup of bell peppers, carrots and purple raw cabbage each

1/2 teaspoon of nutmeg powder

1/2 cup black pepper powder

1 1/2 tablespoon of coconut oil (vegan) or ghee (Clarified Butter)

1 inch ginger grated.

Steps

1. Take a medium-large iron skillet and place it on heat. Add in the coconut oil or ghee and let it melt in the heat.

2. Then add plantain and Chinese long beans and saute until the edges of plantain turn slightly golden brown which means they are cooked. It should take anytime between 8-10 minutes on medium heat. Keep turning upside down every 3 minutes.

3. Add all the remaining veggies, spices, salt and stir fry well for about 3-5 minutes and then add the pre-cooked wild rice.

4. Toss well. If you desire, squeeze some lime juice on top and serve hot — Yummy one pot dish for dinner with loads of veggies, proteins and vitamin rich wild rice. Use the same recipe for other wild rice dishes. Replace plantain with breadfruit, parsnips or even jack fruit. (Note - jack fruit will take a bit longer time to cook and when the fiber texture of jack fruit breaks apart it is a symptom of it being well cooked)

Mint Cilantro Rice

This is one of my daughters favourite !!!!

SERVES
3

METHOD
SAUTE

MINUTES
15

DIFFICULTY
6/10

Ingredients

1/2 cup of chopped fresh cilantro

1/2 cup of chopped fresh mint

5 slices of Serrano peppers

½ inch piece of ginger

1/2 cup of freshly grated coconut.

1 teaspoon mustard seeds

½ cup of peanuts

1 tablespoon of coconut oil

½ teaspoon of asafetida

3 cups of basmati rice cooked and cooled

1/4 teaspoon of black pepper

Steps

1. In a blender blend mint, cilantro, serrano peppers, ginger, black pepper and grated coconut all together into a coarse paste.

2. Now place a large skillet on heat and pour the coconut . Then add the mustard seed and let them crackle.

3. Then add the peanuts and asafetida wait until the peanuts turn crispy and slightly dark brown. Now gently add the cilantro mint coconut paste and sautī.

4. Add the cooked rice and salt and gently mix well, toss upside down making sure that all the greens are evenly spread with the rice and cilantro mint rice with crispy peanuts is ready. (Mix in a way that you don't break the basmati rice)

Lali Lemon Rice

SERVES
4

METHOD
SAUTE

MINUTES
12

DIFFICULTY
4/10

Ingredients

2 cups of cooked Basmati rice

1 teaspoon black mustard seeds

1/2 teaspoon black pepper powder

1/2 cup of dried coconut powder

5 to 8 curry leaves

1 teaspoon white split urad

1/2 teaspoon of asafetida

1/2 cup of fresh cilantro chopped

1 tablespoon of coconut oil

1/2 teaspoon of turmeric powder

1 lime squeezed

Steps

1. Place a medium skillet on heat. Add the coconut oil and wait until it comes to a hot temperature. Add the mustard seeds and let it crackle. Now add the split white urad dhal, curry leaves and let it sautī for 4-8 seconds.

2. Now add the cooked rice, black pepper powder and salt. Mix well and turn off the heat.

3. Then add the fresh lime juice, coconut powder and freshly chopped cilantro and mix well once again. The tangy, yummy Lali lemon rice is ready.

Wonder

Recipes

Vegettie Spaghetti

SERVES
4

METHOD
BOIL

MINUTES
25

DIFFICULTY
7/10

Ingredients

5 ripe tomatoes

3 zucchini

1 teaspoon Italian seasoning

5-8 fresh basil leaves

2 tablespoons of olive oil

1/2 teaspoon black pepper powder

2 teaspoons of cornstarch

1/2 cup of coconut milk

Steps

1. Blanch the tomatoes and peel off the skin.

2. Blend it in a blender to a fine puree. Now pour it in a medium skillet, add another one cup of water and boil it for 10 minutes on medium heat.

3. While the pasta spaghetti sauce is cooking, use a vegetable spiral blade and turn the zucchini into noodles. (Cut the noodles if they are very long) Now turn off the heat and add fresh basil leaves — Italian seasoning, salt, pepper powder and olive oil in the sauce.

4. Now mix the coconut milk and cornstarch. (Add 1 tablespoon of water if needed)

5. Add it to the tomato sauce while continuously stirring. Now add the zucchini vegettie and mix well. Do not cook them in the sauce. They have to be slightly raw, and the heat of the sauce is just enough for it.

6. In the image, I have used some gluten-free spaghetti along with organic zucchini.

Children want to pick out the vegetables so found this recipe very helpful.

SERVES
2

METHOD
SHRED

MINUTES
10

DIFFICULTY
4/10

Gajendra Gobi Aloo

Ingredients

2 cups of shredded cabbage.

1 cup of shredded cauliflower.

1 cup of shredded carrots

1/2 cup shredded bell peppers.

1 cup of potatoes chopped in to small cubes.

2 tablespoon of coconut oil (vegan) /ghee(clarified butter)

4 slices of serrano peppers.

1 teaspoon mustard seeds.

2 teaspoon cumin seeds.

1 teaspoon asafetida

1/2 teaspoon turmeric powder

1/4 teaspoon nutmeg powder

2 teaspoon of coriander powder.

A pinch of cayenne pepper powder.(Optional)

1/2 cup of chopped fresh cilantro.

Steps

1. Place a medium-large skillet on heat. Pour 2 tablespoon of coconut oil /ghee. To test if the oil/ghee is heated to the right temperature, put few mustard seeds, and once they crackle, reduce the heat to low.

2. Start adding the spices, first mustard, wait until they crackle, followed by cumin seeds, pepper slices, asafetida, turmeric powder and sautī for 5 seconds and then add the potato cubes and stir fry for 5 minutes and then close the lid and let it turn slightly golden brown on low heat.

3. Using the cooking spoon, try to pierce a cube of potato to test if it's cooked. Once it's soft and tender, now add all the shredded veggies, in the following order with an interval of 3 minutes. (You may increase the heat a little bit)
First shredded cauliflower& bell peppers and then shredded cabbage and carrots.

4. Now add salt to taste. Toss well on high heat for 5 to 8 minutes. Observe veggies turning slightly tender & juicy but not overcooked, just as shown in the image. Now add the cayenne pepper powder (without garlic) and coriander powder. Turn off the heat. Garnish with fresh cilantro. Serve with Indian flat bread aka Roti.

Balaram Brusell Broccoli

DIFFICULTY
4/10

SERVES
3

MINUTES
15

METHOD
SAUTE

Ingredients

2 cups of brussel spouts sliced into half

2 cups of broccoli chopped medium large size

1 cup of bell peppers chopped into medium
square size.

2 tablespoon olive oil (Vegan)/ butter

2 carrots chopped

2 inch piece of ginger

1/2 teaspoon black pepper powder

1/2 a cup freshly chopped parsley

Steps

1. In a food processor put the carrots, ginger, parsley, and black pepper powder and blend coarsely. (Not fine paste)

2. In a large iron skillet, put the Olive oil(Vegan)/butter on medium heat.

3. Add the sliced brussel and sautī for 5 minutes, then add the broccoli and sautī for another 5 minutes, then add the bell peppers along with the carrot ginger gravy and mix well(add salt) and cook for another 3 minutes on high flame and turn off.

4. The veggies must be sightly cooked, but crunchy not soft or overcooked. A side dish with soups or breads.

Bitter Melon Curry

Bitter melon is an amazingly healthy vegetable which is good for everyone. Here's a special curry which turns is good for tongue as well as the body.

Ingredients

3 cups of bitter melon sliced

1/2 cup of almonds soaked overnight half a cup of freshly grated coconut

2 Teaspoons of paprika

2 teaspoon of coriander seeds

1 tablespoon of tamarind fruit / tamarind Pulp

3 Teaspoon of black mustard seeds

2 tablespoons of sesame oil or coconut oil

5 curry leaves

1/2 a teaspoon of asafetida

DIFFICULTY
6/10

SERVES
4

MINUTES
25

METHOD
SAUTE

1. First in a blender add the soaked almonds, grated coconut mustard seeds, coriander seeds, paprika, one teaspoon of black pepper pods,   tamarind and a cup of water.
2. Blend it until it turns into a fine creamy paste.
3. Now take a medium-large skillet place it on heat and add coconut oil or sesame oil. Put in the mustard seeds and wait until they crackle.
4. Now add the curry leaves and asafetida. Sautī for about 3 to 5   seconds. Toss all the chopped bitter melons into the skillet and mix well tossed them upside down about 5 to 8 times.
5. Add salt mix well and close the lid for about 5 to 8 minutes let it   simmer on medium heat.
6. Open the lid and then add the nice coconut almond sauce you just made into the skillet, add another 2 cups of water, mix well, close the lid and let it cook for about another 8 to 10 minutes.
 7. Open the lid and with the spoon, check if it is nice and tender. Once the bitter melon curry is cooked serve it hot with brown rice wild rice or white basmati rice.

SERVES 3	**METHOD** SAUTE	**MINUTES** 20	**DIFFICULTY** 5/10

Chayote Spinach Dry Curry

Ingredients

2 cups of chayote chopped into medium cubes
1 cup of baby spinach chopped
1 cup of almond powder
1 teaspoon of white pepper powder
1/2 teaspoon of turmeric powder
2 ripe tomatoes chopped into four cubes
2 teaspoons of coriander seed powder
1 1/2 tablespoon of coconut oil

Steps

1. Place a medium large skillet on heat. Pour in the coconut oil. After it comes to heated temperature toss the tomato. Keep stirring and sautī them for about five minutes until the tomatoes are completely cooked.

2. Now toss in the chayote and add salt and white pepper powder. Stir well tossing upside down 3-4 times. Close lid and let it simmer for about 5-8 minutes. (Add a little bit of water if needed) open the lid and turn off the heat.

3. Add the chopped baby spinach,almond powder, coriander seed powder and mix well. The chayote dry curry is ready.

Serve with flat bread/ Gluten free flat bread.

Okra Stirfry

SERVES
2

METHOD
STIRFRY

MINUTES
20

DIFFICULTY
5/10

Ingredients

2 cups of okra washed dried sliced cross ways (shown in the image)

2 teaspoons of carom seeds

1/2 teaspoon of asafetida

1 tablespoon of coconut oil

5 nos curry leaves

1/2 cup of sesame seeds roasted and ground it into dry powder

1/2 teaspoon turmeric powder

1 teaspoon white pepper powder

1/2 cup of fresh cilantro chopped

1/2 lime freshly squeezed

Method

1. Take a medium-size skillet and place it on heat. Then pour in the coconut. Then add carom seeds, asafetida, turmeric powder, and curry leaves. Sautī for 3 -5 seconds.

2. Now add the okra and toss them upside down for about 5 to 6 times making sure all the seasoning is well mixed and the okra is well coated with the coconut oil, do not cover with a lid while cooking okra.

3. Because okra releases its sticky nutrition and then gets absorbed into the vegetable and some of it might stick at the bottom. Keep tossing them continuously on high heat for about 2 to 3 minutes.

4. Then lower the heat and continue tossing.

5. In less than 15 minutes the okra should be nicely steamed, and cooked. Do not overcook okra as it loses its nutrition.

6. Turn off the heat and add the white pepper powder and the remaining spices.

7. In the end, garnish with freshly chopped cilantro,sesame seed powder and lime juice squeezed. It's a beautiful veggie dish as a side dish with a big menu for lunch/a serve for dinner with flat bread or gluten-free flat bread.

Vasudev Veggie Burger

SERVES
4

METHOD
SHALLOW FRY

MINUTES
45

DIFFICULTY
6/10

The Ingredients

4 cups of fresh shredded collard greens

2 cups chick pea flour (Besan)

1/2 cup corn grits

1/2 cup rice flour

1 inch ginger grated

2 tablespoon black pepper powder

1 tablespoon turmeric powder

3/4 cup of white sesame seeds

1 teaspoon asafetida

1/2 a cup melted butter/olive oil.

1 teaspoon garam masala.

1 teaspoon baking powder.

Coconut oil (vegan) / Ghee (clarified butter) to shallow fry.

1. In a large mixing bowl add the shredded collard greens with all the spices and salt and cover the bowl and leave it aside for 10 minutes.

2. With the spices and salt added to the greens, they leave out their flavorful juice which is the base to mix the remaining dry ingredients.

3. After 10 minutes open the lid and add flours, sesame, corn grits, melted butter/olive oil, and baking powder and mix well. Let is set for another 5 minutes.

4. After 10 minutes, heat an iron skillet, pour 1 tablespoon of olive oil/coconut oil (vegan)/ ghee (clarified Butter)on the pan.

5. Now using a round cup spoon/ice-cream spoon, pour the batter in small quantity making 4 burgers at a time.(Medium heat). Pour 1 teaspoon ghee/olive oil/coconut oil on each burger.

6. Wait for 3-4 minutes and then flip it and let the other side turn golden brown as shown in the image. (Your cook time may differ depending on what kind of pan you use).

7. Repeat the procedure for remaining batter.

Serve hot with Mint Tomato Chutney. You may also use burgers with breads and veggies, sauce and cheese. They taste great.

Potato Spinach Subji

SERVES
3

METHOD
SAUTE

MINUTES
20

DIFFICULTY
6/10

Ingredients

2 cups of golden potato peeled and chopped into small size cubes

2 cups of spinach chopped

1/2 inch piece of ginger grated

1/2 teaspoon of black pepper powder

1/4 teaspoon of chili powder

1 teaspoon of mustard seeds

1 teaspoon of cumin seeds

1/2 teaspoon of asafetida

2 tablespoons of coconut oil

1/2 teaspoon of turmeric powder

1/2 tablespoon of coriander powder

Steps

1. Place medium-size skillet on heat. Wait until it is well heated and add the coconut oil. Now add the mustard seeds and wait until they crackle or pop. Add the cumin seeds and asafetida followed by grated ginger. Sautī for 5-8 seconds.

2. Now add the chopped potatoes and mix well making sure the coconut oil is well coated on the potatoes.

3. Keep mixing and tossing every 3 to 5 minutes making sure the potatoes don't get stuck at the bottom and get burnt.

4. Once the edges are slightly golden brown, add the turmeric powder and salt and mix well once again. Now you may close the lid for about 3 to 5 minutes.

5. Then open the lid and pierce one potato with a spoon or a fork to check if they are cooked and tender. Now add the chopped spinach and mix well 3 to 4 time on medium heat let it cook on medium heat for another 2 to 3 minutes.

6. Turn off the heat. You don't want the spinach to be cooked fully, you want it to be steamed and retain its green fresh color and flavor.

7. Add the coriander powder and mix well once again, garnish with half a cup of fresh cilantro and a dash of lime. Serve it hot with the flat bread.

Jack fruit Mini Burgers

SERVES
2

METHOD
BLEND, FRY

MINUTES
40

DIFFICULTY
6/10

Ingredients

3 cups of canned jackfruit squeezed out all the water. If you are using fresh jack fruit boil them for about five minutes and drain the water and squeeze all the excess water.

1/2 cup almonds

1 teaspoon of mustard powder

1 teaspoon of paprika powder

2 cups of rice flour

2 tablespoon of coconut oil

1 cup of freshly chopped cilantro

1 teaspoon of minced Serrano pepper

1/2 teaspoon of white pepper powder

1 teaspoon of asafetida

1. In a large mixing bowl put in all the sliced raw jack fruit and mash it with your hands in such a way that you have all the fibrous texture of the jack fruit nicely separated. Now add the rice flour and salt to this and let it sit for about five minutes with close the lid.

2. Meanwhile add the almonds, mustard seeds, pepper in a spice blender and turn it into a fine powder. Add it to the mashed jack fruit.

3. Toss in all the fresh cilantro. Now add all the remaining spices and the oil and mix it well so that it turns into a softball, and the jack fruit fiber is not runny and is like that of a flat bread dough.

4. Now make about 10 to 15 equal sized balls and press it in between your palms   making flat medium sized burgers.

5. Now place a medium-large iron skillet on heat. Pour one tablespoon of coconut oil or regular olive oil (not virgin).

6. Now press the jack fruit balls down on the pan making them into small burgers of about 1 cm thickness, make 4 to 5 burgers at a time, wait until the sides turn golden brown or slightly darker.

7. Turn upside down to the other side, if needed add another tablespoon of oil. Once they are dark and golden brown on both the sides and look crispy take them out of the skillet and repeat the same procedure for all the remaining burgers.

Serve it hot with the mustard cilantro dip (check Chakra Chutney Corner)

SERVES
6

METHOD
SAUTE, SIMMER

MINUTES
40

DIFFICULTY
7/10

Jack fruit Curry

Ingredients

3 cups of raw jack fruit chopped. In this recipe I have used canned raw jack fruit as it is difficult to find fresh raw jack fruit in the western countries.

If you are using fresh jack fruit it just increases the cook time of the jack fruit at least by 5 to 10 minutes

2 tablespoons of coconut oil

1 1/2 cup of freshly grated coconut

3 Kashmiri Lal mirch/ 2 teaspoon paprika

1 tablespoon of mustard seed for the gravy

1 teaspoon mustard seeds for the seasoning

1 tablespoon full of seedless tamarind pulp

1 tablespoon of coriander seeds.

1 teaspoon of asafetida

1 teaspoon of black pepper powder

Steps

1. First, prepare the gravy for the jack fruit.

2. In a blender add grated coconut, kashmiri lal mirch or paprika, asafetida, tamarind, 1 tablespoon of mustard seeds, coriander seeds, black pepper powder and 1 1/2 cup of water. Blend it until it turns into a very fine paste.

3. Now place a medium, large skillet on heat. Pour coconut oil and wait until it's heated. Toss the 1 teaspoon of mustard seeds wait until they crackle.

4. Now toss the chopped jack fruit into the seasoning. Mix /toss well until the seasoning is well coated on the jack fruit. Add salt mix once again and close the lid.

5. Let it cook on low heat for 10-15 minutes. (until semi-tender).

6. Then open the top and pour in the coconut mustard gravy, add another cup of water . Mix well and close the lid and let it cook in the sauce soaking some of the flavor full spices of the gravy for another 8 to 10 minutes with closed lid. Serve it hot with wild rice/white rice or flat bread.

Suran Almond Curry

Suran Almond Curry

The elephant foot also known as Suran is a beautiful vegetable found in India has its great significance in the Vedic text of ayurveda. Suran is advised into your diet when a person suffering from digestive issues the fiber present in this vegetable acts as an excellent colon cleanser.

Ingredients

3 cups of chopped elephant foot or suran

1/2 cup of soaked almonds overnight

1/2 cup of shredded coconut

1 teaspoon black pepper powder

1 teaspoon paprika

2 teaspoon coriander seeds.

1 tablespoon of tamarind pulp

1 teaspoon mustard seeds

1 teaspoon cumin seeds

8 to 10 curry leaves

2 tablespoon of coconut oil

SERVES 5	**METHOD** BLEND, SAUTE	**MINUTES** 35	**DIFFICULTY** 7/10

1. Take a large skillet place it on heat.

2. Pour in the coconut oil and let it heat for 5 to 10 seconds on medium heat. Add the mustard seeds to the oil and let it crackle. Then add the cumin seeds and curry leaves.

3. Now add the chopped elephant foot vegetable.

4. Stir well on medium heat for about 5 minutes . Close the lid let it simmer for about 5 to 8 minutes.

5. Now in a blender add the almonds, coconut, black pepper powder, coriander seeds, tamarind pulp and 2 cups of water and blend it into a very fine paste.

6. Now open the lid. Pour in this nice tamarind coconut almond gravy that you made and add a little water if needed. Then add salt to taste and stir well.

7. Now let it cook for 10-12 minutes or until tender with closed lid. Serve hot with brown rice. /

Dosa Dharma Taco

With the basic principles of Ayurveda, Dosa Dharma Taco is a combination of rice and split black gram savory pancake stuffed with most healthy purple potato subji drizzled with lime and sesame seeds., Which makes it a complete meal for lunch or dinner. The exotic looking yummy purple potatoes have several health benefits. All potatoes are naturally high in potassium, which helps regulate blood pressure. But the extra antioxidants in purple potatoes make them even more effective than other varieties of potatoes. A medium-starchy texture, making them versatile and suitable in most recipes that call for potatoes.

Dosa Dharma Taco

SERVES
6

METHOD
SOAK,BLEND,SAUTE

MINUTES
50

DIFFICULTY
9/10

Ingredients

For the savory pancake aka Dosa.

3 cups of raw basmati rice

1 & 1/4 cup of split black gram (white urad dal)

1 teaspoon fenugreek seeds.

2 cups of puffed rice.

2 teaspoon Himalayan pink salt.

Ingredients

For the Purple potato subji

10- 14 small purple potatoes boiled, peeled and sliced into half.

1/2 teaspoon fresh ginger grated.

Small serrano pepper chopped.

3 teaspoon white sesame seeds.

2 tablespoon coconut oil.

2 teaspoon cumin seeds.

1/2 teaspoon asafetida.

1/2 cup freshly chopped red bell Peppers.

1/2 cup freshly chopped cilantro.

2 teaspoon freshly squeezed lime juice.

Steps for the Pancake /Dosa

1. Wash and soak black gram & fenugreek seeds. Then add the puffed rice in the end to this and soak all together for 8 hours. Also, soak the rice separately for 8 hours.

2. After 8 hours of soaking grind black gram, fenugreek and puffed rice together into a very fine paste and grind rice a bit coarse separately.

3. Then mix all together keeping the thick pancake batter consistency and let it ferment for 8 to 10 hours in a warm temperature preferably inside the oven turned off. This process should be done the previous day of when you plan to make Dosa Dharma Taco.

The natural process of fermentation that takes place in the batter is perfect for your digestive system as per Ayurveda as it increases the bioavailability of nutrients and minerals present in the food. Lactic acid formed during the process of fermentation not only preserves the food but also helps promote healthy gut bacteria for a healthy intestinal flora. Plus the bacteria present in the process of fermenting helps breakdown the proteins and supports the liver absorb all of it almost like a predigested food or like taking in some probiotics along with food.

After 8 to 10 hours you will see the batter raised with some bubbles. Now your batter is ready.

Prepare for the gorgeous looking Purple potato subji before making the dosa.

1. Heat the coconut oil in a medium size skillet and add cumin seeds, asafetida, ginger, and sliced serrano peppers and sautī for 10 seconds. Now add the sesame seeds and red bell peppers and sautī for another 3 minutes.

2. Then add the purple potatoes and mix well, add salt to taste and keep mixing its until evenly hot and cooked well into the species. (approximately 5 to 8 minutes on medium heat). Turn off the heat and garnish with freshly chopped cilantro and lime juice.

Note:

1. Drizzle some extra sesame seeds on top if you like and sprinkle some cayenne pepper powder if you would like it to be extra hot in taste.

2. If you would want to avoid the lengthy procedure such as waiting for 8 hrs for fermenting, you can try the same recipe with Mahadev Moong Dosa.

Now begins the exciting part :) preparing the DoSa DHaRmA Taco.

1. Heat a pan and pour one large rounded spoon full of batter on the pan (spread it a little bit if needed) and drizzle in some coconut oil and let it cook for 3 minutes until the top part looks cooked/dry and the bottom is golden brown as seen in the image.

2. Then put a large spoonful of Purple potato subji in the center and gently lift from the corner and fold into half as seen in the picture and press gently for the stuffing to be firm and not fall out when lifting it entirely off the pan. Then gently lift and place it on a large plate and garnish with some extra cilantro and desired spices as you like.

Cucumber Idli

| SERVES 4 | METHOD SOAK, STEAM | MINUTES 60 | DIFFICULTY 8/10 |

Ingredients

3 medium size cucumbers (peeled and shredded).

3 cups of Idli Rava (cream of rice).

1 cup of coconut milk.

1 cup of freshly grated coconut/dry coconut powder.

2 tablespoons coconut oil to grease the idly plates

Steps

1. In a large mixing bowl, put in the shredded cucumbers and add salt, leave it for 15 minutes with a closed lid. The salt will allow the cucumber to release its fresh, flavorful cucumber water which will be the base to mix all the remaining ingredients and soak the idli rava(cream of rice).

2. After 15 minutes add all the other ingredients except coconut oil (it is for greasing the idli plates). Now mix well, add water if needed and let it soak for another 20   minutes with a closed lid.

3. After 20 minutes, prepare the idli cooker. Add water in the lower container and place it on heat for boiling. Then grease all the idli plates with coconut oil nicely.

4. Then fill the batter until half in each individual cup. (let there be some cucumber water along with the batter when you pour in each cup) now put it on steam in the pot. Now let it steam for 20 minutes on medium high heat.

Serve it warm with pumpkin chutney. Check the Chakra Chutney Corner for the recipe

Mahadev Moong Dosa

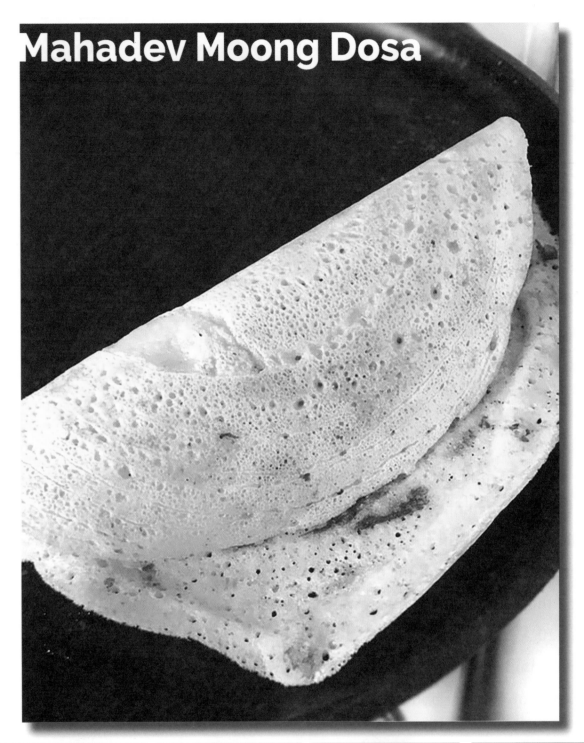

SERVES
8

METHOD
BLEND,GRIDDLE

MINUTES
10

DIFFICULTY
2/10

A protein rich savory pancake

Ingredients

2 cups of split yellow moong beans aka Dal.

3/4 cup of Basmati rice.

1 teaspoon cumin seeds.

1 inch slice of fresh ginger.

1/2 teaspoon turmeric powder.

1/4 teaspoon asafetida.

5 slices of Serrano pepper

1/2 a cup freshly chopped cilantro

Steps

1. Wash, rinse and soak moong dal and rice overnight. Next day morning grind the soaked grains with all the other ingredients in to fine batter, the consistency should be that of a dosa or pan cake batter and then add freshly chopped cilantro mix well.

2. Now heat a cast iron pan on medium flame for 15-20 seconds. Grease it with coconut oil and gently wipe off with cotton wash cloth.

3. Then pour a large spoonful(use a sizable rounded cup spoon)of batter on the pan and then starting from the center , in clockwise direction gently spread the batter with a gentle pressure just enough for it to spread round and thin using the same spoon.

4. Wait for 3 minutes and pour some ghee/coconut oil/olive oil with a spoon all around the dosa in clockwise directions. The sign that its baked/cooked well is that it turns slightly   yellow/golden color as shown in the image and leaves the pan from the edges. Use a flat spoon and lift it up by first working on the corners and then gently slide the spoon to the center and lift it up.

5. Repeat the procedure for as many dosas you would like to make. Serve with purple chutney

Veggie Chips

SERVES
3

METHOD
FRY

MINUTES
35

DIFFICULTY
2/10

Ingredients

2 purple potatoes.

2 medium size yam.

Coconut oil (vegan) / Ghee (clarified butter) for frying.

Salt & black pepper powder for seasoning.

Wash and slice the potatoes and yams with a slicer and then put them in hot water for 5 seconds and put them all on a dry washcloth and wipe it all dry and leave them for 10 minutes to air dry. Now fry them at about 370° F until edges turn dark and they look crispy. Place them in a bowl, season them with pepper and salt. (you can also add plantain, sweet potato, and Idaho   potatoes and make a variety of chips)

Kunti Quinoa Pulav

An easy way to have the quinoa supergrain

The Ingredients :

2 cups of Tri color quinoa

1 tablespoon of coconut oil(Vegan)/ ghee(-clarified butter)

1 teaspoon cumin seeds

1 teaspoon grated ginger

5 slices of Serrano pepper

2 dry bay leaves

2 medium size cinnamon bark

1/2 cup finely chopped green beans

1/2 cup finely chopped cabbage

1/2 cup finely chopped broccoli

1/2 cup finely chopped cilantro.

Pinch of turmeric and asafetida

1/4 teaspoon nutmeg powder

1/4 teaspoon cinnamon powder

1/2 cup finely chopped carrots

SERVES	**METHOD**	**MINUTES**	**DIFFICULTY**
4	BOIL, SAUTE	25	5/10

1. Boil 2 cups of tri-color quinoa in excess water until soft and tender but not overcooked. Drain the excess water and keep aside. (approximately 10 minutes boiling time)

2. Now put a large cooking pan on heat. Add 1 tablespoon of Coconut oil (vegan)/ ghee (clarified butter). Add cumin seeds, bay leaves, cinnamon bark, slices of serrano peppers, ginger. Toss all the spices for 15   seconds and then add pinch of turmeric and asafetida.

3. Add the chopped green beans and carrots first and cook them in the seasoning for 5 minutes, then add cabbage and broccoli and cook for another 3 more minutes, then add salt and boiled quinoa, a pinch of cinnamon powder and nutmeg powder and mix well.

4. Keep tossing veggies and quinoa to for next 5 minutes on medium heat. Then close the lid for another

3 minutes on low heat. Open the top and garnish with freshly chopped cilantro.

Hari Hari Hummus

SERVES
6

METHOD
BOIL, BLEND

MINUTES
50

DIFFICULTY
4/10

A simple home made Hari Hari Hummus is great to dip with veggie chips, tortilla chips or even with a cheese grill sandwich.

Ingredients

2 cups of Garbanzo beans (soaked over night & pressure cooked until soft.)

2 cups of freshly chopped parsley

1 small sized serrano pepper

1 inch piece of ginger

2 tablespoon lime juice (freshly squeezed)

1 tablespoon honey

1/2 a cup of olive oil

Salt as needed

1/2 cup of water (remains from the water used for boiling the garbanzo beans)

Steps

1. In a food processor first add ginger, serrano pepper, 1 tablespoon boiled garbanzo beans and water and process until smooth paste.

2. Now combine all the ingredients except the parsley and process once more.

3. You don't want the garbanzo to be like a paste, and it should be slightly coarse as shown in the image.

4. In the end, add the fresh parsley and pulse grind until its nicely mixed and coarsely ground. Adjust water to have the desired consistency.

 SERVES 6	 METHOD SOAK, PAN FRY	 MINUTES 40	 DIFFICULTY 6/10

Alarnath Instant Appam

Instant Appam. This is an instant version of south Indian dish which consists of split black gram(urad dal), rice & puffed rice soaked, grind and ferment overnight. The specialty of the recipe is the pan in which it is made. The Appam pan! (Mine came from India, you may try finding it at your local Indian store or online). I wanted to try an instant recipe which turned out great in taste with added veggies and spices.

Ingredients

Semolina (rava) 2 cups

1 1/2 cup yogurt

2 cups of warm water

1/2 cup of freshly grated coconut /dry coconut powder

2 teaspoon ENO fruit salt

For seasoning : 1 tablespoon coconut oil, 1 teaspoon mustard seeds, 2 teaspoon split black gram(urad dal), 3 to 4 slices of serrano paper, 5 curry leaves, pinch of asafetida

1/2 cup of the following veggies grated /finely chopped

1/2 a cup carrots

1/2 a cup bell peppers

1/2 a cabbage

Steps

1. Take a large bowl and soak the semolina (rava) in yogurt and warm water, whisk it well and let it sit for 15 minutes.

2. Then add the veggies, grated coconut /dry coconut powder and salt to taste.

3. Now time for seasoning. Pour 1 tablespoon of coconut oil in a heated pan, add the mustard seeds and urad dal. Wait until all mustards seeds crackle and urad dal turn golden brown. Now add 3 to 4 slices of serrano pepper and curry leaves. Wait 5 seconds for the spices to cook and infuse the flavors, in the end, add the asafetida and immediately turn off the heat and pour the seasoning in the batter. (at this point if you feel the batter is too thick you may add a little water, the consistency of the batter is as same as the idly batter) Now add the ENO fruit salt, and mix well.

4. Now its time to make the Appams. Heat the appam pan and grease it well with coconut oil. Pour the batter in each little cup (half of its depth) of the appam pan. Wait for 3 minutes for it to cook on one side and then gently turn it upside down very slowly. If it is cooked well on the bottom side, it will be effortless to flip, and it will not break apart, and you get a perfect round Appam. :)

Serve it with tomato mint or coconut chutney. (For recipe check the Chakra Chutney page)

Cucumber Dosa

Everyone eats cucumbers in salads, yogurt Raita (Indian Yogurt Salad) or pickled as a side dish with sandwiches. How about a delicious Pancake aka Dosa which tasted like fresh cucumbers?

Yes, that's what is Cucumber Dosa filled will freshness, delicious cucumbers inside with other spices and greens. Try it for breakfast, I m sure you will love it! According to ayurveda cucumber controls pitta or excess heat in the body. Good for joints and bones. Very hydrating for skin & eyes.

SERVES
6

METHOD
SOAK, PAN FRY

MINUTES
50

DIFFICULTY
7/10

Ingredients

2 medium size cucumbers

2 cups of Semolina

1/2 a cup freshly grated

3/4 cup dry coconut powder

1/2 cup freshly chopped cilantro

1/2 cup chopped Indian curry leaves

1/2 teaspoon asafetida

1 tablespoon coconut oil

Salt to taste

Note: For gluten free option you could use Corn meal and 2 teaspoon of corn starch and follow the same recipe.

Steps

1. In a large mixing bowl shred the cucumbers and add salt, asafetida, grated coconut and cover with a lid, keep aside for 20 minutes. Salt will allow the cucumbers to release all the flavorful cucumber juice which will be the base for all the remaining ingredients.

2. After 20 minutes add all the remaining ingredients and mix well. (add water if the batter and not runny)

3. Now place a medium-large iron skillet on heat. After 5 to 8 minutes pour 2 tsp of coconut oil and wipe/spread evenly all over the pan. Your pan is ready to make the cucumber dosas.

4. Now take a handful of batter as shown in the image (in the next page) and place in the center of the pan, then spread it evenly, pressing down on the pan with your hand gently making a 1/2 cm thick dosa.

5. Let it cook for 3 to 5 minutes by pouring 1 teaspoon coconut oil on the top side and then flip it down to cook the other side, both the sides should turn golden brown as shown in the image on the next page. Repeat the procedure for as many dosas you would like to make. Serve with Purple Chutney. (For recipe check out the Chakra Chutney Corner)

Bulgur Bisi Baath is a healthy version of Bisi Bele Baath, a traditional dish in Karnataka, India. A very delicious combination of veggies, spices & pulses with a unique seasoning. Here in my recipe, I have replaced rice with organic red burger wheat. Hence it called Bulgur Bisi Baath. Best served as lunch or dinner.

Bulgur Bisi Baath

SERVES
6

METHOD
BOIL,SEASON

MINUTES
40

DIFFICULTY
8/10

Ingredients

2 cups of Red Bulgur Wheat/ Gluten free option Whole buckwheat groats

1/2 a cup split yellow moong beans(moong Dal)

1/2 a cup Toor Dal /Pigeon Pea (split)

1/2 a cup split chickpea (Channa Dal)

1 cup freshly grated coconut/dry coconut powder

3 tablespoon Coconut oil (Vegan)/ Ghee (Clarified Butter)

1/2 cup of Tamarind soaked in warm water for 30 minutes/2 tablespoon of lime juice

2 tablespoon of grated Indian Jaggery (Raw sugar)

1/2 a cup freshly chopped cilantro

Salt to taste.

Following vegetables 1/2 a cup each chopped.

Tomatoes, green beans, fresh green peas, carrots & potatoes.

Spices to make the Bulgur Bisi Baath masala

1 teaspoon mustard seeds

3 teaspoon cumin seeds

2 teaspoon fenugreek seeds

2 tablespoon coriander seeds

1 teaspoon black pepper pods,

1 inch cinnamon bark

2 whole cloves, 2 teaspoon asafetida, 1 teaspoon chili

powder(optional), 1 teaspoon turmeric powder, 3 teaspoon paprika

powder for a nice color as seen in the image.

Spices to do the seasoning

2 teaspoon mustard seeds, 1/2 cup peanuts, 1/2 cup split cashew nuts, 1 teaspoon asafetida, handful of fresh curry leaves.

Steps

1. Wash and rinse all the pulses, bulgur wheat and pressure cook in 6 cups of water using a rice cooker, open the lid and add all the vegetables and salt. Add another 2 cups of water.

2. Meanwhile, heat a medium-size skillet and put coconut oil(Vegan)/ Ghee (Clarified Butter)

3. Then start adding the following spices with 5 seconds interval and sautī them lightly, fenugreek seeds, mustard seeds, cumin seeds, black pepper pods, cinnamon bark, cloves, coriander seeds and turn off the heat.

4. The spices should not burn or turn brown. Just slightly roasted. After the spices cool down, put them in a blender with freshly grated coconut and tamarind pulp and blend into a fine paste. Add water as needed.

5. Now add this blended spices to the cooked grains and mix well. Add salt as needed. Add the jaggery and bring it to boil once again.

6. Its time for the seasoning now, heat a small skillet, pour 2 tablespoon coconut oil (vegan)/ ghee(clarified butter), to check its on right temperature by sprinkling few mustard seeds and see if they crackle sound. Then add all the mustard seeds, nuts, asafetida, and fresh curry leaves and pour it on the Bulgur Bisi Baath. Mix well and garnish with freshly chopped cilantro.

Tips: You can also add 1/2 cup of black eye beans if you like, soak them overnight.

Bamboo Veggie Stirfry

An exotic veggie like bamboo shoots should never be overcooked with too many spices, keep it simple, relish its real taste and wonderfully chewy texture and fragrance. Along with great taste, it also consists of so many health benefits. Its very good for weight loss, helps balance your cholesterol levels, and boosts the immune system. It also has cancer-fighting and anti-inflammatory properties. It is heart-friendly and contains protein and very good for people with diabetes and heart patients.

SERVES
2

METHOD
SAUTE

MINUTES
15

DIFFICULTY
4/10

Ingredients

2 cups of fresh Bamboo shoots

(chop all the veggies thin and long like the bamboo shoots as seen in the image)

1 cup of chinese long beans

1/2 cup of purple cabbage

1/2 cup of regular cabbage

1/2 cup of carrots

1/2 cup of almond flour

1 tablespoon of black pepper powder

1 tablespoon of grated ginger

1 tablespoon of oilve oil/ almond oil(Vegan) / ghee(clarified butter)

2 tablespoon of honey

2 tablespoon of lime juice freshly squeezed

Steps

1. Heat a large skillet and pour olive oil/almond oil(Vegan) /Ghee (clarified butter)

2. First add the bamboo shoots & Chinese long beans and stir fry for 5 minutes.

3. Add a little salt and continue stir-frying on a high flame for 3 minutes or until you see the bamboo shoots edges turn slightly golden brown.

4. Now add all the remaining veggies and salt, pepper powder and grated ginger, toss them well and stir fry for 3 more minutes.

5. Other veggies remain raw not overcooked.

SERVES
2

METHOD
FOOD PROCESSSOR

MINUTES
30

DIFFICULTY
5/10

Yogi Energy Bars

Ingredients

1 1/2 cup of dates

1/2 cup of cashew nuts

1/2 cup of almonds

1/2 cup of walnuts

1/2 cup of carob powder

1/2 cup of Chia seed

3 tablespoons of coconut oil

Steps

1. Roast dates in half a tablespoon of coconut oil for about 3 to 5 minutes on medium heat. Then let it cool down. Transfer it into the food processor.

2. And next roast all the nuts separately in half a tablespoon of coconut oil for about three minutes until they turn slightly golden and look crispy. "Do not roast the Chia seeds and the carob powder".

3. Now let the nuts cool down. Add all the nuts, carob powder, and chia seeds into the food processor with the dates. Process until all the nuts are coarse and well mixed into the dates as shown in the image.

4. Take a parchment sheet and transfer the processed nuts and dates mixture on it and place another sheet on top of the mixture then take a rolling pin and roll it flat like about a half a centimeter or 1 cm thickness.

5. Place it into a baking tray and refrigerate for about 45 minutes. Take it out and use a pizza slicer and slice them into the desired size/shapes could be diamonds, rectangles or squares.

6. Place them into an airtight glass container by using baking sheets in between to avoid sticking. Keep refrigerated. You can preserve this in the refrigerator for at least a week. Have it in the morning or afternoon but no nuts after sunset, difficult on digestion.

Gluten free base Param Pizza |||

Param Tava Pizza ||

Param Pizza I

The healthy Pizza series begins

SERVES
2

METHOD
BAKE

MINUTES
60

DIFFICULTY
5/10

Ingredients

2 cups of all purpose flour

1 cup of oats flour half

1 cup of flax meal

10-15 fresh basil leaves

1 teaspoon baking powder

1 teaspoon baking soda

1 teaspoon Italian seasoning

2 tablespoons olive oil

1/2 cup of whole wheat flour

6 tomatoes ripe

1/2 cup black olives sliced

1/2 cup of broccoli chopped with crowns

1/2 cup of zucchini sliced

1/2 cup of asparagus sliced

1/2 cup of mixed bell peppers chopped

Vegan Cheese or cheese as needed

First, we will make the tomato sauce with fresh tomatoes

1. By slightly making cuts on tomatoes skin blanch the tomatoes for 5-8 minutes and then peel off the skin. Now blend tomatoes into a fine puree in a blender.

2. Put this fresh puree into a skillet and let it cook for about 15 minutes until it goes little thick like a tomato sauce. Now to this fresh tomato sauce add two teaspoons of cornstarch mixed in a little bit of water to give it a fine texture to spread nicely on the pizza. Now add black pepper powder, salt and fresh basil to this sauce. Your pizza sauce is ready.

3. Now it's time to make the base of the pizza which is yeast free. Take a large mixing bowl, add all the flours, Italian seasoning baking powder, baking soda and one cup of olive oil and mix well evenly making sure all the oil is evenly mixed in the flour.

4. Also, add salt to taste and mix well now slowly adding water to knead it into a nice firm dough like that of any bread. Let it sit for about 15 to 20 minutes covered with a lid so that the dough is soft.

5. Now take a rolling pin and roll it into a nice thin Pizza base crust and the edges slightly turned inwards.

6. Pour the sauce in the center and spread to the edges. Then sprinkle all the good cheese on the sauce and then followed by all the wonderful veggies.

7. Drizzle some olive oil and preheat the oven on 380º F Bake for about 25-30 minutes and broil for 2 minutes till edges turn slightly brown, and cheese turns golden brown on the top. Take the pizza out from the oven and sprinkle some fresh basil leaves and some black pepper powder.

8. Repeat the procedure to make more pizzas with the remaining dough and sauce.

Param Tava Pizza

SERVES
3

METHOD
BAKE

MINUTES
1 HR

DIFFICULTY
5/10

Ingredients

2 cups of all purpose flour

1/2 cup of Chia seeds

1/2 cup of oats flex meal/flour

1 cup of rice flour

3 teaspoon of Italian seasoning

1/2 a teaspoon of black pepper powder

10 to 15 fresh basil leaves

1 teaspoon of baking powder

1 can of artichoke hearts sliced

1 cup of Brussel sprout sliced

1 cup of green and red bell peppers sliced

8 to 10 slices of fresh Serrano peppers

2 tablespoon olive oil

1 tablespoon mixed olive oil and coconut oil to grease the tava/cast iron pan

Cheese(Vegan or regular) as needed

Param Tava Pizza

Steps

1. For the pizza sauce, we will use the same recipe as in the pizza I. Now prepare the base of the pizza. In a large mixing bowl put all the flours, chia seeds, baking powder, 1 tablespoon of italian seasoning with two tablespoons of olive oil and mix well making sure the oil is evenly spread all over the flour.

2. Now little by little add some water to the flour and make it into a nice dough as good as the bread dough, soft and fluffy and let it set aside for 15 to 20 minutes with closed lid.

3. Please heat the oven to 380° F.
The specialty of this pizza is that it is made in a cast iron skillet.

4. Now make equal size rolls, about 4-5 rolls of the dough.(2 inch diameter) Grease the skillet with mixed coconut and olive oil all the way bottom and to the edges. Coconut oil is a natural non-stick element to your baking so that your pizza doesn't get stuck on the cast iron skillet.

5. Now press one roll of dough starting from the center going towards the edges of the skillet into a nice evenly spread pizza base and gently squeeze (roll up a little) the edges so that it holds the sauce and the cheese in the pizza (so that it doesn't overflow)

6. Now spread one large rounded spoonful of tomato sauce on the base. Sprinkle the desired amount of cheese on the tomato sauce and then arrange the wonderful artichoke hearts and the other veggies as like shown in the image.

7. Sprinkle some black pepper powder if you like it

8. Bake it in the oven for about 25 - 30 minutes or until the edges turn brown and the cheese on the top turns golden brown. Your tava pizza is ready.

Param Pizza III

SERVES
4

METHOD
BOIL

MINUTES
1 HR

DIFFICULTY
5/10

The Ingredients

2 cups of rice flour

1 1/2 cup of tapioca flour

1/2 cup of Chia seeds

1 teaspoon of Italian seasoning

1 teaspoon of baking powder

2 tablespoon of olive oil

1/2 cup of flax meal flour

Himalayan pink salt to taste

1/2 cup of fresh basil leaves

A cup of brussels sprouts sliced into half

1 cup mixed bell peppers chopped

The pizza tomato sauce recipe is the same as that for the
pizza number | and ||

Vegan Cheese/Cheese as needed

2 teaspoon of coconut oil

Step

1. For the pizza sauce follow the same recipe as in for the Param Pizza I and Param Pizza II (Param Tava Pizza).

2. Now prepare the pizza dough which is gluten-free batter as a base for pizza. In a large mixing bowl add all the flour, Italian seasoning, Himalayan pink salt, baking powder, and mix well. Now using a whisk slowly add water to the flour make the batter to the consistency of a pancake batter.

3. Now preheat the oven at 380° F. Use a cast iron skillet and grease it with some coconut oil.

4. Coconut oil gives natural non-stick effect to the skillet so that your pizza doesn't get stuck on the iron skillet but also bakes it crispy, crunchy crust.

5. Now after greasing the skillet pour two spoons (using a medium round headed spoon)of batter in center and let it set by itself by spreading all the way to the edges. If it doesn't then pour a little more and wait for 10-15 seconds for the batter to flow from center to the edges touching all the corners of the skillet.

6. Now bake it in the oven for about 10 minutes or until just the top layer turns dry. Take the skillet out of the oven.

7. Its time to pour the tomato sauce followed by the desired amount of cheese then add all the wonderful veggies such as brussel sprout, artichokes, bell peppers, asparagus, pineapples whatever you would like.

8. Bake it in the oven for another 15 minutes or until the edges turn brown and the pizza cheese on the top turns golden brown(as shown in the image). Please take out the skillet of the oven and use a thin flat spoon, slide it from the edges working around the edges and going to the center and lift it and place it on the wooden chopping board , use a pizza slicer and then slice it into four.

Repeat the procedure for the remaining batter and the sauce you have. It should make at least four small pizza or two large pizzas.

Param Pizza IV

SERVES
4

METHOD
BAKE

MINUTES
1 HR

DIFFICULTY
5/10

Ingredient

For the base

2 cups of buckwheat flour

1 cup of boiled quinoa

2 potatoes boiled peeled and mashed

2 tablespoon of olive oil

2 teaspoon of Italian seasoning

10- 12 fresh basil leaves chopped

Paneer grated or needed / want or make it vegan, please use vegan cheese

For the pizza sauce, recipe remains the same as the Param pizza I , II and III.(avoid corn starch in the sauce for this one)

Choose the toppings of veggies As desired. look at the image of the recipe for some cool ideas.

Cheese or Vegan Cheese as needed

230

Steps :

To make the base

1. In a large mixing bowl. Mix buckwheat flour, mashed potato, boiled quinoa, olive oil, Italian seasoning, add salt.

2. Add a little water if needed. Form a nice firm dough. Now make 3 or equal size ball. Place one the center on Pizza baking tray. Pressing the dough firmly slowly work it around to the corners. Slightly thick about less than a centimeter thickness.

3. Preheat the oven on 380 F and bake the base for about 10 minutes. Take it out of the oven, let it semi-cool and then spread the sauce and sprinkle all the panner followed my desired toppings.

4. Form a beautiful arrangement as shown in the image. Sprinkle some shredded paneer (recotta cheese)or Vegan Cheese. Bake for another 25 minutes or until the crust looks crispy and topping looks slightly burnt on the top layer, take the pizza out of the oven and sprinkle fresh basil leaves. Slice it. Serve hot.

Moringa Falafel Splatters

SERVES
6

METHOD
PAN FRY

MINUTES
50

DIFFICULTY
6

Ingredients

1 cup of fresh Moringa leaves

2 cups of overnight soaked garbanzo beans

1/2 cup of basmati rice soaked overnight

1 inch piece of ginger

1 small size Serrano pepper

1 teaspoon of coriander seeds.

1 tablespoon of olive oil

1/2 cup of corn starch

Coconut oil to shallow fry the splatters

Ingredients for the chutney

1/2 cup of moringa leaves

1/2 slice of medium size Serrano pepper

1 teaspoon of coriander seeds

1/2 teaspoon of cumin seeds

5 almonds

1 tablespoon of dry coconut flakes/ shredded coconut

1 tablespoon of coconut oil

2 teaspoon lime juice

Steps :

First, prepare the chutney.

Place a medium size skillet on heat and pour in the coconut oil. Wait for 5-8 seconds then add cumin seeds and coriander seeds. Wait for 3- 4 seconds for it to crackle then add the moringa leaves and sautī until they are dark in color and slightly crispy. It should take about 3-5 minutes. Turn off the heat. Wait for few minutes for it cool down then add the almonds, shredded coconut and Serrano pepper and put all together in the blender with an added cup of water, lime juice and salt. Blend until fine and creamy (chutney)

Now prepare for the moringa splatters.

1. Put the soaked garbanzo beans and rice in a food processor and process slightly fine. Add the olive oil, ginger, Serrano pepper and coriander seeds.

2. Process again for 2-3 minutes. Now add salt and the fresh Moringa leaves, salt and cornstarch and final process it for 2-3 minutes. Take this mixture out in a bowl and set aside.

3. Now place an iron skillet on heat, wait for 10-15 seconds for it to heat. Turn on the vent and pour in one tablespoon of coconut oil. Using a small ice-cream scoop, scoop a spoon full of the moringa bean mixture and place it on the pan and gently press making it to 1 cm thickness like a splatter, do not worry about what shape it makes. Make 4 to 5 splatters at a time on the pan. Now let it cook until edges turn brown and looks crispy. Gently lift with a flat spoon and turn it upside down. Let the other side cook crispy.

4. Repeat the procedure for the remaining moringa bean mixture. Serve it hot with the chutney. Images on Next page

Moringa Splatters

Moringa Splatters

Day 1

8 am Golden kiwi (or green kiwi) chia lemonade or green kiwi.. 22

1 pm Golden kiwi chia mint chia detox lemonade.... 22

6 pm Ginger mint chia detox lemonade   23

Day 2

8 am Strawberry chia detox..... 25

1 pm Mango/pineapple chia detox..... 26

6 pm Ginger mint chia detox lemonade..... 23

Day 3

8 am Blueberry chia detox lemonade 25

1 pm Nectarine detox lemonade 28

6 pm Mango chia mint detox lemonade..... 26

Day 4

8 am Strawberry chia detox lemonade..... 25

1 pm Turmeric cardamom chia detox lemonade..... 30

6 pm Ginger mint chia detox lemonade..... 23

Day 5

8 am -Cumin fennel tea..... 34
10 am Pineapple chia detox lemonade..... 26

1 pm Blueberry chia detox lemonade..... 25

5 pm Cumin fennel tea..... 34
7 pm Raspberry blackberry chia detox..... 24

Day 6

8 am Cardamom Chamomile tea..... 38
10 am Golden kiwi chia detox lemonade 22
1 pm Cardamom chamomile tea..... 38

3 pm   Mango mint chia detox lemonade..... 26
6 pm   Blueberry chia detox lemonade..... 25

Day 7

 8 am Cardamom chamomile tea..... 38
10 am Avo celery almond smoothie..... 51

1 pm Raspberry blackberry chia detox lemonade..... 24

3 pm   Mango mint chia detox lemonade..... 26

6 pm   Mint ginger chia detox lemonade..... 23

Day 8

8 am Orange zest tea..... 38
9 am Kriya kichiri..... 149

1 pm Barley Soup no black pepper added..... 109

6 pm   Sprout Soup (some black pepper added)..... 113

Day 9

8 am Ginger Fennel tea..... 40
9 am Apple sauce..... 87

1 pm Butternut squash soup..... 107

Day 10

8 am Green shakti..... 30
9 am Apple sauce..... 87

1 pm Prana sprout salad..... 91

6 pm Barley soup..... 109

Day 11

8 am Orange zest tea..... 38
9 am Antibiotic smoothie..... 68

1 pm Broccoli soup..... 102

6 pm Pumpkin soup and cumin fennel tea..... 116 & 34

Day 12

8 am Cardamom chamomile tea..... 38
9 am Antibiotic smoothie..... 68

1 pm Bottle gourd soup and Prana sprout salad..... 111 & 91

6 pm Pumpkin soup and Chamomile cardamom tea..... 116 & 38

Day 13

8 am Cumin fennel tea..... 334
9 am Blueberry walnut smoothie..... 53

1 pm   Sprouted fenugreek spice balls and Barley soup...... 82 & 109

6 pm Bottelgourd soup (if you don't find bottlegourd, use zucchini instead and apply the same recipe as bottlegourd soup..... 111

Day 14

8 am Green Shakti..... 30
9 am Yogi bar with desired tea..... 219

1 pm   Prana sprout mint tomato   soup with desired salad..... 113

6 pm Butternut squash soup..... 107

Day 15

8 am Ginger Fennel tea..... 40

9 am Blueberry walnut smoothie..... 53

1 pm   Kunti Quinoa Pulav..... 201

6 pm Pumpkin soup and Chamomile cardamom tea..... 116 & 38

General Guidelines on Diet

1. Mornings are best for having herbal teas, lemonades, smoothies, and fruits.

2. Try to keep a sufficient gap between drinking lemonades, smoothies and having a full meal.

3. Do not mix fruits with meals. It is not right according to ayurveda.

4. Mid or late afternoon is the best time for a good lunch.

5. As the saying goes if you feel like "To eat or not to eat," better not to eat.

6. To cook your own food and to eat is a million times better than eating store bought food or in restaurants. The main reason being in both cases they will try to add the cheapest ingredients to save money and compromise on your health.

7. Cooking your own food, cleaning might seem like a chore, but it will benefit you million times over than eating out.

8. When you prepare and eat your own food, you eat your own consciousness.

9. Do not eat heavy at night, It causes obesity and slows down the functions of the body.

10. Try to drink as much water in between meals. Avoid drinking water immediately before or after or during meals.

Glossary

Ayurveda - The ancient Indian science of healing

Yoga - The ancient Indian science of connecting body, mind and soul

Prana - Life energy

Mukunda - A name of the Supreme Lord meaning one who gives liberation

Kunti - A very famous queen from the Mahabharata, mother of pandavas.

Hari Hari - A name of the Supreme Lord

Alarnath - A form of the Supreme Lord who is very merciful

Appam - South indian name for cooked rice balls

Gajendra - Name of an ancient elephant who became a devotee of the Lord

Vasudev - The name of Supreme Lords father as per vedic literature

Yogi - One who practices Yoga

Chandrayana Vrata - A 30 day fasting based on the phases of the moon

Ekadasi - The 11th day either from new moon or full moon considered auspicious for fasting

Shakti - Sanskrit word for energy

Ghee - Clarified Butter

Taittariya Upanishad - A book which is a part of the ancient vedic knowledge which deals with the five layers of our body food, energy, mind, intelligence and the soul.

All recipes are vegan

Below are the ones with gluten and vegetarian options

The following contain gluten

Baked Samosa..... 130

Barley soup..... 109

Alarnath Instant Appam..... 206

Bulgur Bisi Baath..... 212

Param Pizza |

Param Tava Pizza ||

The following have vegetarian options

The Yogic scriptures mention the khichris to be had with Ghee (Clarified butter), but vegans could use coconut oil instead of ghee

Rice Moong bean Kichiri

Qunioa Khichri

Chayote Kale Khichri

Wild Rice Stir fry

Gajendra Gobi Aloo

Balaram Brusell Broccoli

Vasudev Veggie Burgers

Veggie Chips

Bamboo Veggie Stir fry

All the pizzas, Vegetarians could use regular cheese and Vegans could use vegan cheese

Testimonials

ALOHA, I thank Food For the Soul for cooking all the meals for all the meals here in the teacher training in Hawaii. Prepared with love and care. Yogis understand that food comes from mother earth showing true love for us. The sun and the moon show true love for us unconditionally. You can see Sundari who prepared this Food For the soul has prepared it with Love, the main ingredient in the food was love, it purifies the body, purifies the mind. I am grateful that I had this experience this food for the soul for the last 14 days

Yogi Charu
Yoga Instructor, New York City, USA

I had the pleasure to take part in 300YTT where Sundari was preparing our meals for 2 weeks. We had a delicious selection of teas, smoothies, juices, soups and pizzas, salads, Kichiri, veggie pasta and so much more. All the recipes were vegan, Ayurvedic and prepared specifically for after fasting to nourish our bodies, minds, and souls. At the time I was 7mo pregnant, and Sundari made sure that I received all the nutrients I needed to nourish not only my body but the life growing in my belly as well. I have a chef for a husband, so I am not easy to please, but I can't recommend Sundari enough. As my teacher says, the most essential ingredient in any food is love. And Sundari put her heart in her dishes. I wish her all the best and looking forward to purchasing her new cooking book.

Vesela Mincheva
RYT, LMT
Kona, Big Island Hawaii

I just wanted to say that I have fallen IN LOVE with the Book FOOD FOR THE SOUL. All the recipes you have created are tasty and healthy. My blood sugar is normal, I feel more energetic, my thoughts are purer after the diet you have suggested. The Best part is the number of options you have in Vegetarian/Vegan space, it's tough to find a good variety of food in Vegetarian/vegan cuisine, and you provided healthy and delicious options.

- Pankaj Bhardwaj, Software Professional, Pittsburgh, USA

Aloha Everybody, My name is Dave. I have a recipient of 14 beautiful days of Food For the soul, It has changed my anatomy, thinned my waistline and changed my whole concept of what I want to put into my body. I wanna thank Sundari, the wonderful creator of Food for the soul

David Michael Dunham
CEO Oahu Luxury Homes LLC
Honolulu, Hawaii, USA

I have been the recipient of guided fasting mentioned in the above book. Thank you to the authors of Food for the Soul book for presenting such timeless precious techniques to cleanse our body. I did the liquid diet fast for 7 days. After fasting, I can feel that I am more energetic and lighter. I lost about 10 lbs as well. Interestingly one of my doctors also said that this type fasting process will detoxify the body, reset the whole system and generate new stem cells that have more immunity and are disease resistant. So modern science is also accepting the benefits of ancient ayurvedic principles. I am grateful to the authors for a fantastic piece of work for the welfare of mankind. I strongly recommend everyone to get this book and try the fasting Yoga to see amazing results. Thank you!

Sowmya Chennuri
Software Professional, Houston, USA

I had the privilege of spending two weeks from Food For The Soul. Food For the Soul is beautiful based on the Ayurvedic system of cooking. Everything is holistic and Organic. Everything here is so fresh that you can feel the Prana in everything. I am really grateful for that whole entire experience because for me my body is my temple. Food for the soul. Grab your copy now.

Kate Kuss
Yoga Trainer, New York, USA